Recommendations for

For over two decades, it has been Wolfi Eckleben in church planting .... ne not only understands and practices *The Art of Loving Well*—he practices and understands the art of leading well. In his life and ministry, both loving and leading people have been inexorably connected. I am grateful for his leadership and friendship. I pray that this book upgrades your relationships and impacts the way you lead at home, at church, and at work.

Steve Murrell
Co-founder & President, Every Nation Churches & Ministries

I have applied these truths in my own life to diffuse some rather 'prickly' and awkward situations. I have also used them to encourage many others to do the same, right from my pre-teens to the managing directors and senior management teams I have worked with. The principles in this book are truly universal and life-changing! I'd highly recommend you read it.

Liz Lugt
Organisational Culture Consultant, Movation Leadership

The Art of Loving Well is not another simple how-to manual leaving out the more complex issues of the inner man/woman to be addressed for real meaningful relationships to exist. The ten Arts Wolfi lays out will help you to develop the character and skills necessary to grow and sustain the relationships we all long for. In this world struggling with loneliness, it's the ability to get along and finding the relational well-being that leads to the good life, and *The Art of Loving Well* is an excellent part of the solution to those problems. Read and enjoy.

Russ Austin
Lead Pastor Southpoint Community Church, Jacksonville, Florida

Wolfi is a leader I respect greatly, especially in his life-long commitment to student mission and discipling the next generation. Research tells us that is it now normal for young people to experience broken and unreconciled relationships within their family and friends, and I have found this to be particularly true in my work with university students. I love that this book seeks to address this very current, crucial and powerful challenge we are all facing in how to do relationships well. I also love that Wolfi actually lives what he writes, this isn't just theory, this is hard-won wisdom from a pastor who has been serving people in real relationship for decades.

Miriam Swaffield
Global Student Mission Leader for Fusion

One cannot teach what you have not embraced in your own life. Wolfi is a true artist in painting a practical picture of "Loving Well". One line truly lit up the page: *"Consuming is never as lifegiving as contributing. We were created for more than that."* The Art of Loving Well truly is a lifegiving contribution to anyone wanting to build their own character to love better!

Leon & Zania Schoeman
Directors of Broadcasting - TBN UK, TBN EU & TBN in Africa

The truths in this book are life changing. Not only have I found this in my own life, but I have also seen this in the lives of others with whom I've shared these principles. Recently even a brief conversation with colleagues made all the difference to their usual family dramas at Christmas time. I have seen how applying these principles has helped stop the pattern of unhelpful interactions with loved ones and even averted a few people giving up and walking away from a friendship or relationship or it is breaking down completely. I would highly recommend you pick up the paintbrush of *The Art of Loving Well* and give it a go!

Audette James
Physiotherapist, Team Leader at Every Nation London

Wolfgang has written one of the timeliest books on relationships. Reading this book inspired, challenged, and coached me to work on my relational climate with the people God has placed in my life. This book will be a timeless classic and it will impact thousands of people, and I know that it will also be a great blessing to you the reader.

Willem Nel
Visionary Leader of Every Nation Faith City, executive life coach, motivational speaker, and author of *A Silent Adventure* and *Making the Impossible Possible*.

Jesus told us to love one another as He has loved us. This book will help anyone do just that! Rooted in scripture, and filled with personal anecdote and prompts to action, *The Art of Loving Well* will help individuals not only understand themselves better, but also grow in receiving and giving love. I believe this book will positively impact marriages, family life, church community, and every other kind of relationship. Loving well is good news! It's the heart of God.

Joanna Chee
Author of *Forever Loved: Eve's Story*

THE
ART
OF
LOVING
WELL

Ten powerful ways
to change your relational climate

WOLFGANG ECKLEBEN

AN EVERY NATION LONDON PUBLICATION

TITLE: The Art of Loving Well

Copyright © 2018 by Wolfgang Eckleben

May 2023 Edition

For information contact:
6 Staveley Gardens, London, W4 2SA, United Kingdom
www.everynation.london
www.wolfinlondon.com

ISBN Number:
- 978-1-9999-8045-0 Paperback
- 978-1-9999-8046-7 eBook

Cover design: Amy Eckleben

DEDICATION

To my wife Ali.

For our incredible life and love shared.

Contents

Foreword

A rt conjures the idea of expensive, non-essential and only for the rich and famous. And there is a grain of truth to that. Sometimes loving well is viewed the same way – an expensive, non-essential for those who have the time and energy in this busy world we live in.

My friend Wolfi Eckleben dispels this notion. He proposes that loving well is an art that is of great value but is not out of reach. I read most of the manuscript of this book on subway rides. Straight to the point, rich, yet concise it can be read on the way to work.

In between controlled giggles (not to annoy my fellow-passengers), moments of contrition and getting fresh insights; it was altogether a refreshing read.

While not all of us will be artists of the painting and sculpting kind, we can all learn to be artists of the loving well kind. This book can help us get there.

By Joey Bonifacio

Senior Pastor at Every Nation Church Singapore. Member of the Global Leadership Team of Every Nation Ministries.
Author of five published books, including *The LEGO^R Principle.*

Acknowledgements

I've been privileged to have many teachers and fellow students on this journey:

My first very special thank you must go to my amazing wife Ali, who first introduced me to some of these truths, and for loving me enough to allow me to learn to grow in Loving Well. We've tested these Arts on the front line of our marriage, our family, and our leadership, and are definitely experiencing the positive benefits of the resulting climate change.

A talk at the Global Leadership Summit[149] by Joseph Grenny[150] many years ago about *Moments of disproportionate influence* sparked my curiosity about the massive difference that learning and applying relational skills can make.

In 2014 I attended an Emotionally Healthy Skills conference presented by Pete and Gerry Scazzero in London, and this, together with some of their excellent books helped me to see

the clear link between emotional health and spiritual maturity, setting me on a passionate pursuit of what I started calling *The Art of Loving Well*. I highly recommend their resources at www.emotionallyhealthy.org.

I must give a huge shout-out to all the fantastic people who make up the incredible Every Nation London church, where we have been teaching these truths for several years and together have embarked on a whole new Loving Well adventure which is slowly becoming culture.

A special thank you to Wes Hinsley and Jo Chee, for your very constructive feedback, input, and suggestions on the manuscript. The book is definitely a better read because of your valuable contributions.

Thank you to my amazing daughter Amy for another great cover design.

Thank you to Fiona Matier, for your meticulous proofreading and final touches, giving me the confidence to say it's done.

Thank you to my God, who first loved me. And loves me. And you.

And thank you for choosing to read this book. Let's go on a Loving Well adventure and change our world one relationship at a time.

Inviting you to Love Well

Because to Love Well is to Live Well

T he following statements express some of what I believe about love and what it does and can do. Have a slow read through these and consider whether you would agree:

Love is the most powerful transforming force on this planet.

Everything good grows when love grows.

Growing in love is the most significant growing we can do.

To Love Well is to Live Well.

Our lives flourish as our love flourishes.

Our ability to love well is the most accurate measure of our maturity.

I am convinced this is all true about love. It's in loving that we truly start living. But what does it really look like to love others? How do I do that? How do we do that *"well"*?

LOVE IS FOR EVERY RELATIONSHIP

Love is not just for romance, but for every relationship in our lives. When talking about love in this book, I'm applying it in the broadest sense to all our relationships:

Our friendships
Our family
Our colleagues
Our dates
Our spouses
Our teammates
Our churches
Our enemies
Our neighbours
Everyone, really.

I am convinced that the more we grow in Loving Well, the more all our relationships will thrive and flourish, and the more our lives and the lives of those around us will flourish.

Sadly, it's also true that:

> *When love isn't as it should be, then most of life won't be what it could be.*

And, *Without love we are nothing. Zilch. Zero.*

If this is true, then ouch! But it also presents us with a great opportunity: If we are nothing *without* love, just imagine what we could be *with* love! If we could learn to Love Well, much could change. That is what we will explore through the truths in The Art of Loving Well. My aim in this book is captured so well in this prayer of the great Apostle Paul:

> *So this is my prayer:* **that your love will flourish** *and that you will not only love much but well. Learn to love appropriately. You need to use your head and test your feelings so that your love is sincere and intelligent, not sentimental gush.*[2]

To flourish means that something is "growing or developing in a healthy or vigorous way, especially as the result of a particularly favourable environment".[3] It means "to abound, increase and overflow, to exceed by going beyond the expected measure".[4] That sure sounds like the way I want to live. How about you? If yes, then I invite you to join me on this journey of learning to Love Well.

Perhaps you're facing some challenging relational situations right now and have picked up this book out of a measure of desperation. There is no magic wand to fix every difficult relationship, but these truths will always be a part of the solution for you. Learn them and start living them and believe for a miracle where you need it.

Perhaps your relationships are generally in a good place now, but you know that there is more, and good is often the greatest enemy of best. Applying these truths has the potential to transform your good relationships into the great relationships you yearn for.

We all want flourishing lives, but sadly many of us live in relational climates that are not conducive to much flourishing, and in pretty much every environment, there are things to learn that could cause healthier, happier, and more fulfilled relationships. And if love is as crucial as I am suggesting, then our lives can only flourish fully if our relational climate is healthy.

YOU CAN MAKE A DIFFERENCE

The good news is that we have many choices that can make significant differences in our relationships. We can influence our relational environments, not just be subject to them.

You have choices to change things.

You can decide to learn to Love Well and put what you learn into practice. And as you do, I believe that you will see significant positive results in many areas of your life.

The "how" of all that I want to share with you in this book is probably best summarised in the words of the Apostle Paul:

> *Watch what God does, and then you do it, like children who learn proper behaviour from their parents. Mostly what God does is love you. Keep company with him and **learn a life of love**. Observe how Christ loved us. His love was not cautious but extravagant. He didn't love in order to get something from us but to give everything of himself to us. Love like that.*[5]

As you may have gathered already, I am a believer and follower of Jesus Christ. I only came to faith after finishing school and getting to know and experiencing the love and truth of God since then has been nothing short of life-changing for me. The Bible has a lot to say about Loving Well, including many words from Jesus himself, and it is the value and importance of those teachings that ultimately inspired me to write this book.

While you may or may not believe everything I do, I trust that the principles and practices I share in this book will be a significant help to you in all your relationship challenges and opportunities.

I am a fellow traveller with you on this journey of *learning a life of love*, and I invite you to join me as we learn to Love Well. (And everyone around you will be thrilled that you did!)

My prayer for you as you read and apply the truth in this book is:

> *May the Lord make your love for one another and for all people grow and overflow.*[6]

To Love Well is to Live Well.

Let's learn to do that well.

Our lives can only flourish as fully as
our relational climate is healthy.

We have a
Global Cooling Problem

Because love is growing cold

We have a global warming problem. It's a big deal with potentially grave and destructive consequences.

However, I want to propose that we have another, possibly even more destructive problem, which is what I call *The Global Cooling Problem*. Predicting a phenomenon that would grip the world in the future, Jesus Christ famously declared that *"in the last days, the love of many will grow cold"*. [7] I think that we are in those days of love growing cold. Across the earth, we are more connected than ever online but at the same time more isolated and disconnected than ever from real, fulfilling relationships.

Too often we conduct most of our relational connections from the safety of our screens and keyboards and miss out on growing the healthy relational skills that we all ultimately need to succeed in life, whether at work, play or in love. Superficial, shallow, selfish, and disposable relationships seem to be the norm. Conflict and polarisation are on the increase. Loneliness is at epidemic levels, so much so that the UK Prime Minister even appointed the first-ever "Minister of Loneliness" at the start of 2018.

The Global Cooling Problem is real and needs some serious solutions, especially since most issues in our world are relational problems at their root. It doesn't need to be like this, and in this book, I want to present some solutions that could genuinely change your life and the world around you.

Every environment has a climate, and the climate in any environment determines what will flourish in it, or not. England, where I live, has a different climate to Namibia, where I was born. Certain plants flourish in England but would shrivel up in the dry desert climate of Namibia. Each environment has a climate that is optimal for certain things to thrive but might cause other things to wither away.

Every relational environment you are in also has a specific relational climate:

    With your work colleagues
        Your friendships
            Your university mates

At school
Your family
With your parents
With your kids
In your marriage
At the gym
Your church community
Your church small group
Every team that you are on
At work
At church
On the sports field
Every board you sit on
Your neighbours

The relational climate in each of these environments will determine whether the relationships and individuals will flourish or not.

Your current climate is also a good indicator for forecasting your future. If you can improve your climate today, you will change the forecast for your tomorrow, because the prevailing relational climate in which you live has a significant impact on how well you live. This was borne out by a Harvard Study of Adult Development, which Robert Waldinger, director of the study, summarised as follows:

"The surprising finding is that our relationships and how happy we are in our relationships has a powerful influence on

our health. Taking care of your body is important, but tending to your relationships is a form of self-care too. Close relationships, more than money or fame, are what keep people happy throughout their lives, the study revealed. That, I think, is the revelation." [8]

It is not surprising then that the new commandment that Jesus gave reminds us of what is most important: to *"love one another."* [9]

Love is the optimum climate in which relationships flourish.

When love isn't as it should be, then most of life isn't what it could be.

When love is cold or lukewarm, the relational climate simply is not conducive to anyone flourishing.

Where love flourishes, everything will flourish.

When the relational climate is healthy, everybody can flourish, and everybody wins.

The sad truth though is that the relational climate in many of our friendships, workplaces, families, churches, and marriages is far too cold, or at best lukewarm, for us to truly flourish.

I propose to you that *The Global Cooling Problem* and its detrimental effects can be addressed and reversed by every one of us growing in *The Art of Loving Well.*

WHY LOVE "WELL"?

You may ask why I would feel the need to add the adverb *well* to love? Were the Beatles not right when they proclaimed that *"love is all you need"*?! Yes, but for most of us, the verb *love* needs some amplification. We say *"I love"* far too flippantly. We love pizza and movies and our friends and football and chocolate and our sports team and our family. And Jesus. And in loving everything, have we forgotten what it means to truly love others well?

To Love Well is to love in such a way that the one who is the object of your love genuinely experiences your love. You see, I can say *"I love you"* to my wife Ali, but how does she experience my love? How am I showing her my love? Does she feel loved by me through my actions, my reactions, and the words I say and don't say? It's easy to say that I love my neighbour or my enemy, but how do I? How do they experience my love? Would they say that I have demonstrated love to them in some tangible ways?

Love isn't measured merely by my feeling of it for someone, but rather by the recipient experiencing it from me through my words, actions and attitude. I have Loved Well when others are flourishing because of the way I have loved them.

> *Let us stop just saying we love people; let us really love them, and show it by our actions.*[10]

I propose that your life will flourish in direct proportion to the health of your relational climate. If you learn to set the right relational temperature, you will see some amazing changes in many areas of your life.

Now, I can imagine you thinking: Wolfi, surely that's too simplistic. That's like saying we can reverse global warming if we just all stop eating meat. (Shout out to all my vegetarian and vegan friends!) There are massive problems in the world, and just like

> Your ability to Love Well sets the relational climate to determine how you will flourish in all of life.

making a change to the global warming problem seems virtually impossible, it can often seem the same for many of our relational problems. Is there really any hope, and what can love really do to change that?

If that is your question, then the next part of this chapter is just for you:

NEVER UNDERESTIMATE THE POWER OF LOVE

Love is not just a feeling or emotion. It's a powerful transforming force.

Dr Martin Luther King Jr was right when he said:

> *We must discover the power of love, the power, the redemptive power of love. And when we do that, we will make of this whole world a new world. But love, love is the only way.*

At Prince Harry and Megan's wedding, with an estimated 24 million people in the UK, 29 million in the US, and countless more millions across the globe tuned in to watch, Bishop Michael Curry quoted the late Dr King, and added:

There is power in love.
Don't underestimate it.
Don't over-sentimentalise it.
There is power, power in love.

There is power in love.

The quote comes from his *Loving Your Enemies* sermon delivered at Dexter Baptist Church in Montgomery, Alabama, on November 17, 1957. In it, he proclaims this about the transforming power of love:

Now there is a final reason I think that Jesus says, "Love your enemies." It is this: that love has within it a redemptive power. And there is a power there that eventually transforms individuals. That's why Jesus says, "Love your enemies." Because if you hate your enemies, you have no way to redeem and to transform your enemies. But if you love your enemies, you will discover that at the very root of love is the power of redemption. You just keep loving people and keep loving them, even though they're mistreating you. Here's the person who is a neighbour, and this person is doing something wrong to you and all of that. Just keep being friendly to that person. Keep loving them. Don't do anything to embarrass them. Just keep loving them, and they can't stand it too long. Oh, they react in many ways in the beginning. They react with bitterness because they're mad because you love them like that. They react with guilt feelings, and sometimes they'll hate you a little more at that transition period, but just keep loving them. And by the power of your love, they will break down under the load. That's love, you see. It is redemptive, and this is why Jesus says love. There's something about love that builds up and is creative. There is something about hate that tears down and is destructive. So love your enemies.

Love has within it a redemptive power.

There's something about love that builds up and is creative.

I agree. Love changes things. Love doesn't just fill you with fuzzy feelings. It's a force that makes you whole. And changes your world, and the world.

Perfect love casts out all fear.[11]

When you learn to Love Well, you will begin to live well, and those around you will be blessed and changed too.

"CHRISTIANS" BEWARE

Just a word to those of us who identify ourselves as Christians, or disciples of Jesus: the call to Love Well is, of course, a non-negotiable. Jesus gave his disciples a new commandment, to love one another as he has loved us. This was not his *new suggestion*!

We must rediscover and recommit to the supremacy of the law of love. Loving Well should rise above most if not all things. To love is to act like God because God is love. Without love, we have no testimony of the God who so loved the world (everyone, everywhere) that he gave his only Son.

Love is the most powerful amplifier of the Good News we speak. Without love, the truth we speak will just be an empty clanging noise. Without love, our "good news sharing" is just an off-putting hypocritical message to an already sceptical and cynical world. Love is our final apologetic, and Jesus says that when we love one another, *"all the world will know that we are his disciples"*[12]

Wow. *All the world will know.*

That's why we should learn and grow in Loving Well. Because everything flourishes when love flourishes. Because love is a powerful change agent. Because it's what God did and does and how he commands us to live.

> *Live a lover's life, circumspect and exemplary, a life Jesus will be proud of: bountiful in fruits from the soul, making Jesus Christ attractive to all, getting everyone involved in the glory and praise of God.* [13]

But love doesn't come cheap.

Love always costs.

It requires laying down one's life.

> *There is no greater love than to lay down one's life for one's friends.*[14]

CS Lewis described the high cost of love well in *The Four Loves*, the book in which he explores the nature of love:

> *To love at all is to be vulnerable. Love anything, and your heart will certainly be wrung and possibly be broken. If you want to make sure of keeping it intact, you must give your heart to no one, not even to an animal. Wrap it carefully round with hobbies and little luxuries; avoid all entanglements; lock it up safe in the casket or coffin of your selfishness. But in that casket – safe, dark, motionless, airless – it will change. It will not be broken; it will become unbreakable, impenetrable, irredeemable. The alternative to tragedy, or at least to the risk of tragedy, is damnation. The only place outside Heaven where you can be perfectly safe from all the dangers and perturbations of love is Hell.*

Hell: That's where Global Cooling leads.

Everything: That's what's at stake.

Read on if you think the cost for reversing Global Cooling is worth it, and you want to be a part of the revolution.

> Never underestimate the power of love.

Pause to think and talk about The Global Cooling Problem:

⇒ Do you agree that there is a Global Cooling Problem? Why, or why not? What are some of the symptoms that you observe to come to your conclusion?

⇒ Reflecting on the quoted portion of Dr King's speech in this chapter, what do you find the most challenging part to live out?

⇒ Do you have relationships that are strained, broken, distant, or stagnant, and need some climate change? List these and keep them in mind as you read through the book. Consider how you can apply the content to these particular relationships and situations.

⇒ In response to the truth in this chapter, what is the one thing you can do differently to grow in Loving Well

Growing in the Arts

Because it takes heart and skill to love well

P reviously I said that the good news is that we all have many opportunities to make a significant difference to our relational climates, and in this book, I present ten specific ways through which we can do that. I guarantee that as you commit to growing in these areas, your relational climate will improve, and you will begin to see yourself and others around you flourish.

Growth in any area of our lives always follows the pattern of hearing and doing. Understanding, and then applying.

Revelation, then application. Knowing the truth, and learning the skills required to live it out.

It's a delicate combination of heart and hands.

If you're not convinced of the why, you won't be committed to learning and growing in the how.

You will rarely apply in your life what you don't have a revelation of.

You will rarely succeed at anything if you don't develop the skills required for the task.

There is a big difference between having a desire or intention to do something well and committing to developing the required skills to do something well.

> A skill is a learned ability to do something well
>
> to achieve desired results.

You learn a skill through teaching, training, practice, and repetition.

Sadly, not everyone will be prepared to put in the hard work to grow the required skills to create a healthy relational climate. When it comes to love and relationships, we are often too proud, ignorant, or lazy to develop our skills, so we never grow, and never change.

The fact is that often we need to grow up and realise that in relationships, just like every other area in our lives, those who develop the appropriate skills simply achieve better results than those who don't.

Here are the ten *Arts* that we will cover, and why each is important:

1. The Art of Growing Up
   ✓ *Because it takes maturity to love well*

2. The Art of Building Up
   ✓ *Because love builds up*

3. The Art of Feeling Well
   ✓ *Because what is in you will affect what comes out of you*

4. The Art of Listening Well
   ✓ *Because to be listened to is to be loved*

5. The Art of Speaking Well
   ✓ *Because words are powerful climate change agents*

6. The Art of Engaging Well
   ✓ *Because unresolved issues pollute our relational environments*

7. The Art of Fighting Well
   ✓ *Because we will fight, and need to learn to fight for the sake of relationship*

8. The Art of Forgiving Well
   ✓ *Because we mess up, and will often need to forgive and be forgiven*

9. The Art of Functioning Well

    ✓ *Because relationships flourish when we each do our part*

10. The Art of Living Loved

    ✓ *Because we can only give what we have received*

You may have noticed that the final Art we will look at is *The Art of Living Loved*. This is the ultimate key that enables us to really love others well. Once you have love, you can give love. If you haven't got love, you can't give love.

I put this as the last Art in the book to remind every reader of this vital ingredient before you try and put these other truths and skills into practice. This may seem back to front for you if you are feeling deeply unloved or empty of love right now. If that's you, I would recommend that you go straight to that chapter and start there.

You see, we can only give what we have got.

The good news is that because God in Jesus Christ has first loved us well, we too can Love Well. Because we have his love, we can give his love.

In learning and applying the truths of this book, think of yourself as an artist, and each of these ten areas as a medium available to you for adding to the texture and beauty of the relationships you have around you. Applying them in the right order, in the right combinations, with the right consistency, and in the appropriate doses is much more of an *Art* than it is a science. (And let's face it, *The Science of Loving Well* just doesn't sound right, does it?)

Like many an artist starting out, your first attempts may not be masterpieces. It will require much practice, especially where you have neglected or been unaware of the importance and potential of one or more of the Arts

> **Like many an artist starting out, your first attempts may not be masterpieces.**

available to you. You will need to persevere and practice, but the results will be worth every effort you make.

The good news is that we can all grow and *learn to love appropriately* through *The Art of Loving Well*. As you commit to this, a whole new world of flourishing is waiting for you!

So here's my prayer for you as you read and apply *The Art of Loving Well*:

> *May the Master pour on the love so it fills your lives and splashes over on everyone around you.*[15]

Or to put it another way:

> *May the Lord make your love increase and overflow for each other and for everyone else.*[16]

We *can* learn to Love Well.

So:

> **Don't lose your grip on Love and Loyalty.**
> *Tie them around your neck; carve their initials on your heart.*
> **Earn a reputation for living well** *in God's eyes and the eyes*
> *of the people.*[17]

Let's do that.

As you commit to Loving Well,
there is a whole new world of flourishing waiting for you!

Pause to think and talk about Growing in the Arts:

⇒ Thinking about relational skills, what do you think those close to you would describe as your most positive relational skill or strength?

⇒ Looking over the list of ten *Arts* we will cover in this book, which three initially stand out for you as areas in which you most obviously want or need to improve?

⇒ How loved do you feel right now? If it's more on the empty side, please go ahead and read the chapter on *The Art of Living Loved* first, and then come back to the others.

The Art of Growing Up Well

Because it takes maturity to love well

They say that the biggest room in the world is the room for improvement. And that room is usually in our own house.

All relational climate change starts with me. And you.

We are all growing older. That's inevitable. But the bigger question is: Are we still growing up?

Question: *Are you still committed to growing up?*

To commit to *The Art of Growing Up Well* is to commit to on-going personal development and maturity. This is crucial because our success in relationships can only go as far as our commitment to personal maturity. If we stop growing, then our relationships will suffer.

Another undeniable reality of life is that *"The times, they are a-changin"*.[18] Seasons of life change whether we like it or not; but whether we also grow through those seasons - maturing through them - is for us to think about.

In romantic relationships, I see it this way: God created us *male* and *female*, but it was a *man* who joined himself to his wife. There is a big difference between a *male* and a *man*. Being a *male* is a matter of birth, but being a *man* is a matter of maturity. The same for a *female* and a *woman*.

It doesn't take much maturity to fall in love, but it takes a lot of maturity to stay in love and to keep loving well "for better, for worse, for richer, for poorer, in sickness and in health, to love and to cherish, till death do us part".

Any male and female can get together and cuddle and kiss and have sex, but it takes a mature man and woman to have a strong, lasting, flourishing relationship. It doesn't take much maturity to have sex and produce a child, but it sure requires maturity to raise a child well.

Similarly, it's one thing to have a team, but quite another to become a united, thriving, productive unit. It's one thing to hang out with people, but quite another to build deep, meaningful friendships. It's one thing to go to a church service, but quite another to be the church and *"love one another as I have loved you"*.[19]

Maturity is not a matter of our age but of our actions and choices and is ultimately measured by our ability to Love Well.

Love is not just a noun, but a verb. It's something we do. It's extremely practical. Love without action or expression is useless. It's not just something we feel but something that causes us to speak and act. It's the superglue that keeps relationships together.

> Love without action or expression is useless.

Sadly, we live in a culture of much artificial maturity. Authentic intimacy is replaced by artificial intimacy, where we mistake social media connections with having real friends that we know deeply. In our artificial intelligence age, we mistake our access to vast amounts of information with having real knowledge and wisdom. And social media lets us express our artificial intentions by "commenting", or "liking" or even perhaps "loving" ideas and issues on social media, but it's a poor surrogate for doing something active that will make a difference.

In growing up, we must commit ourselves to be lovers, not lusters.

Lust takes at the expense of others, while love gives even at the expense of self.

Lust is self-focused, while love is others focused.

Immaturity majors in lust, not love.

Maturity is an ingredient that you will find in all stories of love that last, and we find it right at the heart of probably the greatest words about love ever penned: The first letter to the Corinthians, chapter thirteen. This is set right between two very practical chapters about the functioning of the church as a relational body, and this reminds us that love isn't a theory hidden somewhere in deep theology and mystery.

This famous chapter starts with the words: *"If I ... have not love ... I am nothing... I gain nothing...".*

Did you get that? ***Nothing!***

Nothing is what you get when you multiply anything you have with zero. You get zero. Zilch. Nil.

A life without love is nothing.

A church without love is nothing.

A Christian without love is nothing.

A business without love is nothing.

A team without love is nothing.

A community without love is nothing.

That passage continues like this:

Love is patient and kind. Love is not jealous or boastful or proud or rude. It does not demand its own way. It is not irritable, and it keeps no record of being wronged. It does not rejoice about injustice but rejoices whenever the truth wins out. Love never gives up, never loses faith, is always hopeful, and endures through every circumstance.

That's beautiful and powerful! Imagine a relational environment filled with that kind of love!

It's worthwhile for us to read this in a different Bible translation too. I find this helpful because it is so easy to become familiar with what you are used to. You can hear these beautiful words but miss their profound meaning. In the same way, familiarity is one of our most significant challenges to relationships and healthy relational climates.

We so easily become familiar with those close to us, taking them for granted and not even noticing when we begin to drift apart into the shallow and superficial end of a relationship. Or even worse, like the proverbial frog in the frying pan, some people get so used to destructive, toxic and even abusive relational environments that they begin to accept them as their new normal.

Sometimes we need a new perspective on what the climate we are in is really like. For example, at the time I was writing this section of the book, I had a meeting with a few local church leaders in our office lounge. We'd been in there for about an hour with the door and windows closed when someone else came in to join us. As they opened the door, they drew back sharply at the stale air in the room. We'd become accustomed to it in there, but someone needed to remind us that it was time for some fresh air.

So let's read the same passage from The Message Translation:

> *I'm bankrupt without love.*
> *Love never gives up.*
> *Love cares more for others than for self.*
> *Love doesn't want what it doesn't have.*
> *Love doesn't strut,*
> *Doesn't have a swelled head,*
> *Doesn't force itself on others,*
> *Isn't always "me first,"*
> *Doesn't fly off the handle,*
> *Doesn't keep score of the sins of others,*
> *Doesn't revel when others grovel,*
> *Takes pleasure in the flowering of truth,*
> *Puts up with anything,*
> *Trusts God always,*
> *Always looks for the best,*
> *Never looks back,*
> *But keeps going to the end.*
> *Love never dies.*

Wow, that's a high standard! What will it take to love like that? Remember, we're focusing on maturity in this chapter, and the key to this is in the verse that follows these above:

> *When I was a child, I talked like a child, I thought like a child, I reasoned like a child. When I became a man, I put away childish things.*[20]

Notice what he says here:

> *I became a man:* Maturity is a process of becoming. We are all becoming something, for better or for worse.

> *I put away childish things:* To grow up is to put away childish ways. Children only think of themselves; grown-ups are supposed to think of others. To love well requires us to "put away childish things" and be others centred.

The Apostle Paul refers to his maturing in three key areas:

The way he spoke.
Maturity means growing in using words well to express preferences, concerns, hopes and emotions.

How he thought.
Maturity means forming personal opinions that flesh themselves out in living well. You will never outgrow your thinking.

How he reasoned.
Maturity means coming to conclusions about yourself and about life that guide your decisions and ability to make sound judgments about all that comes across your path.

> How we speak, think, and reason is an accurate measure of our maturity.

In my *DateTalk* book (*"almost everything you want to know about relationships, dating, and sex"*), I have a chapter titled *"I'll have a whole one please"*. In it, I assert that *"The best preparation you can make for a future fulfilled relationship, is a commitment to personal wholeness."* In exploring what personal wholeness looks like, I propose that a whole person can confidently make the following statements about themselves:

- ✓ **I have a life** (I'm not looking for others to complete me)
- ✓ **I am unique** (I am not in competition with, nor comparing myself to others)
- ✓ **I am loved** (and so have love to give to others)
- ✓ **I am a man/woman** (I *am not just* a male or female, but am growing up)
- ✓ **I am valuable** (My life is deeply meaningful to others)
- ✓ **I have left** (The negatives of my past are no longer shaping my future)
- ✓ **I am ready for us** (I am prepared to accept the responsibility for a relationship)

When these become our true - not just aspirational - conclusions (reasonings) we are well on our way to maturity and readiness to Loving Well.

It's also vital to have an accurate measure of maturity. We don't measure ourselves by ourselves. Neither do we measure our maturity by comparing ourselves to others. For a Christian, Jesus Christ himself is the standard of maturity, as we see in the Apostle Paul's letter to the believers in Ephesus:

*In the church ...we should no longer be children, ...Instead, we will speak the truth in love, **growing in every way more and more like Christ**, who is the head of his body, the church.*[21]

This, by the way, is what *discipleship* is: The process of growing to become more and more like Jesus, who is the very image of the One in whose image we were created.

Growing Up means looking in the mirror when we are not Loving Well, and asking ourselves some honest self-awareness questions like:

Why did I react like that?

Why was I so irritated/angry/defensive/judgmental/offended?

Why does _____ bother me so much?

We'll explore this further in the next chapter on The Art of Feeling Well.

Maturity also takes responsibility. Just like with global warming, many of us check out. We think that we can't do anything to make a difference to climate change, so we do nothing. We too easily assume or actively assert that our relational challenges are someone else's fault and responsibility. But maturity must take responsibility because you cannot grow out of anything that you will not own.

> Faith cannot fix what you won't face.[22]

To be mature is to take responsibility for all that is growing in the garden of your soul. The good and the bad. The weeds and the good fruit. The Apostle Paul encourages Christians to grow "the fruit of the Spirit":

> ...*the fruit of the Spirit is love, joy, peace, patience, kindness, goodness, faithfulness, gentleness, and self-control.*[23]

Or as The Message Translation puts it:

> ...*things like affection for others, exuberance about life, serenity. We develop a willingness to stick with things, a sense of compassion in the heart, and a conviction that a basic holiness permeates things and people. We find ourselves involved in loyal commitments, not needing to force our way in life, able to marshal and direct our energies wisely.*

He contrasts this good fruit with what grows in a heart committed to its own selfish ways:

> *It is obvious what kind of life develops out of trying to get your own way all the time: repetitive, loveless, cheap sex; a stinking accumulation of mental and emotional garbage; frenzied and joyless grabs for happiness; trinket gods; magic-show religion; paranoid loneliness; cutthroat competition; all-consuming-yet-never-satisfied wants; a brutal temper; an impotence to love or be loved; divided homes and divided lives; small-minded and lopsided pursuits; the vicious habit of depersonalizing everyone into a rival; uncontrolled and uncontrollable addictions; ugly parodies of community. I could go on.*[24]

Ouch!

The fruit from our lives is either growing from what we sowed and cultivated ourselves, or what someone else sowed, and we allowed to grow there. We not only have a responsibility, but also a *response-ability*. We can choose how to respond. Some things may not be our fault but taking responsibility for any weeds now growing in our garden is the only way we will rid our garden of them. We are not helpless slaves needing to accept whatever comes our way.

> We not only have a responsibility, but also a response-ability.

Knowing what to do is a good start but doing what is right is the real measure of maturity. For example, you may be aware of some vital conversations that you need to have about something with a friend, colleague, or spouse, but doing that in a way that grows things up instead of blows things up takes real skill. We'll cover that in *The Art of Engaging Well*.

In the same way, you can know that it is good to forgive others who have hurt or disappointed you, but actually putting The Art of Forgiving Well into practice is often easier said than done and requires some real skill.

The good news is that we can grow up.

We are a work in process. We may not yet be who we want to be or could be or should be, but we don't need to stay as we are. We CAN Grow Up Well!

As you choose to leave childish ways behind, you can experience and express the amazing kind of love that the Apostle Paul wrote about. Perhaps read that great love chapter again. Slowly. This time from The Passion Translation:

> *Love is large and incredibly patient.*
> *Love is gentle and consistently kind to all.*
> *It refuses to be jealous when blessing comes to someone else.*
> *Love does not brag about one's achievements*
> *nor inflate its own importance.*
> *Love does not traffic in shame and disrespect,*
> *nor selfishly seek its own honour.*
> *Love is not easily irritated or quick to take offense.*
> *Love joyfully celebrates honesty*
> *and finds no delight in what is wrong.*
> *Love is a safe place of shelter,*
> *for it never stops believing the best for others.*
> *Love never takes failure as defeat, for it never gives up.*
> *Love never stops loving.*

I'm sure agree that's the kind of love worth pursuing!

So let's commit to leaving childish ways behind.

Let's not just grow older, but let's keep Growing Up Well.

Because all relational climate change starts with me.

And you.

Pause to think and talk about The Art of Growing Up:

⇒ What is the one thing that you found most relevant or helpful in this chapter?

⇒ Are there any childish ways of speaking, thinking, or reasoning that you need to leave behind?

⇒ Which of the "whole one" statements listed are most relevant to your Growing Up journey right now?

⇒ Can you identify any weeds growing in your garden that you have not taken responsibility for?

⇒ If so, what can you do about these?

⇒ In response to the truth in this chapter, what is the one thing you can do differently to grow in Loving Well?

The Art of Building Up Well

Because love builds up

We can choose to be one of three kinds of people in our relational environments:

Breakers,

Boring,

or Builders.

Builders Love Well.

Breakers and the Boring don't.

Let me define these a little further:

The Breakers

Breakers are those who have an innate need to put others down to feel bigger and better about themselves. For various deep-rooted reasons, they tend to feel small in themselves, so they need to make others around them feel smaller. They suck the life out of the room they are in. When you share a hope or dream with a Breaker, they always give you plenty of reasons why it won't work. A Breaker is like an open window on a cold and windy day, causing the temperature in a room to plummet. They complain and consume, but rarely contribute.

The Boring

The Boring ones are those who come into an environment and make no difference or contribution. They are like a thermometer, just measuring what is and adapting to it. They conform. Blend in. They comment or complain about what is but do nothing to change the climate to what it should be or could be. They are the ones who don't say a word or give a smile at the supermarket checkout. They just pass through without any positive influence or impact. They live to neither succeed nor fail. That's being Boring.

When it comes to relationships, Breakers, and the Boring make lousy lovers, and they do nothing to influence the relational environments they are in positively. By "lousy lovers" I mean lovers in the sense of Loving Well, not the dating kind of lovers, since you might not feel like that with your workmates! "Lousy" simply means "very poor", "bad", or "infested with lice", and that alone should put everyone off being a Breaker or Boring!

The Builders

Builders, on the other hand, make a positive difference to their environment. They change things for the better. They invest. They fix. They lift others. They encourage. They bless. They contribute more than they consume.

Builders are not just like thermometers that read and reflect the temperature. Instead, they act like thermostats that accurately read the current temperature, and then actively engage all the Loving Well Art that is at their disposal to achieve the right relational temperature in which all can flourish.

As we look at these, we will probably need to admit that each of us tends to be a mix of all three. But again, we can change, and when we do, our relational climates will change too. The more we can be Builders, the better our relational climate will be, and the more we and everyone around us will flourish.

If we can become more aware of how others experience our presence and our actions, then we might learn some important things - surprises perhaps - about how we can change and grow into better relational builders. Without this awareness, we will rarely be ready to change.

Considering the statements I've made above; how would you answer the following two questions:

Do you think those close to you would generally describe you to be more of a Breaker, a Builder or Boring?

What effect do you have on your relational environments? Do you generally act more thermometer-like, or thermostat-like?

Remember: *You are only as strong as you are honest.*

The good news is that all of us can learn to be builders and thermostats. We do not have to accept the status quo of cold and lukewarm relational climates. We can grow in learning to Love Well and experience the blessing of a healthy relational climate.

WHY DON'T WE BUILD UP?

There are many reasons why we may be stuck as Boring or act as Breakers.

Often it is because deep down we don't believe that we have anything of value to contribute to those around us. Such a mindset needs an urgent change because if you think that you have nothing worthwhile to offer others, you will at best be Boring. Or else you will feel threatened by those around you and react as a Breaker.

YOUR LIFE IS DEEPLY MEANINGFUL TO OTHERS

Something that helped me tremendously with this is making a personal life decision that *My life is deeply meaningful to others.* I try to make this my attitude whenever I walk into a crowd of strangers at a party or conference, or get up to speak publicly, or hang out with friends: *My life is deeply meaningful to those around me.* This truth statement guides my attitude in every relational environment into which I step.

This is not pride (as the Breakers and Boring will often accuse), but merely a recognition that I am on this earth on purpose for a purpose, and I am blessed to be a blessing to others through the gifts with which I am graced.

You may say: *I don't have any gifts. I've got nothing to give. My life definitely does not feel deeply meaningful to others.* This is false.

The truth is that you DO have something to contribute.

You DO matter.

God has uniquely graced you with gifts by which you can be a blessing to those around you.

Your life *is* deeply meaningful to others.

> *We have different gifts, according to the grace given to each of us...* [25]

Our gifts are not the same, they are unique.

To be unique means that you are without rival. There is no one like you. Or like me. I would make an inferior imitation of you, and you would make a poor version of me. You do not need to compete with anyone else, nor compare yourself to them. You are one of a kind, and in your uniqueness, your life is deeply meaningful to others.

> *Be yourself. Everybody else is already taken.*
>
> - Oscar Wilde

Sadly, though all of us are born as unique originals, most people will die as cheap copies, trying to be someone else. Last time I checked, copies are cheap. It's the original that has the highest value, and when you accept your unique original special self, that's when the blessing of your life can flow to others around you. If you struggle to believe and accept this about yourself, please have a good look at the truth I'll cover in *The Art of Functioning Well*.

Another reason why you can't or don't *Build Up* could be that you have grown up or lived too long in an environment filled with Breakers and Boring people. You have been broken down too much, too often. You've been put down. Ignored. Overlooked. Ridiculed. Rejected. Belittled. Labelled. Compared. And your response has been to become less and less of you. Perhaps you have compromised in trying to conform as you seek acceptance and approval at all costs.

Here's a fact: You will rarely flourish in a Breaker or Boring environment. That's why spending time with Builders is so crucial, and why being immersed in an environment full of Breakers and Borings can be so limiting. Yes, you do want to be the Builder positively influencing the Breakers and Boring, but you need Building Up too. If you're not getting enough of that, then I would urge you to begin to prioritise surrounding yourself with a few more Builders.

Builders are those who believe in you and want the best for you. They champion you to succeed. They seem more interested in you than they are in themselves. They make you feel like you can make it. They leave you feeling better when you walk out of the room than when you walked in. This is what Builders do in our lives, and we all need them.

Pause and consider:
- Do you have any Builders in your life?
- Who are they? List a few of them.

Recently my daughter Amy volunteered at a summer youth camp we run in London. One of the things she noticed and that really impressed her was how all the teens seemed to really encourage one another with words. This is the culture we are trying to create in our relational environments, and it's highly attractive and transformative.

This *Building Up* relational climate is one of the key characteristics of the Every Nation movement that I am privileged to be a part of. From years back there has been this habit amongst many leaders of calling each other by names such as "Champ", "Big Faith", and "Hero"! While some may find that a little strange when these words are spoken *with sincerity,* they awaken something powerful in us and among us. We are on a challenging mission together and need all the Building Up we can get and give each other. This Building Up attitude is also a very special part of every Every Nation gathering that I attend, where outsiders coming in often remark how everyone seems to want everyone else to succeed.

There's no bragging and posturing and one-upmanship. We don't compare ourselves to each other, but we encourage and inspire one another. It's a Builder environment, and we all flourish in it. I need it. I love it. I flourish when I hang out with Builders.

I hope that you have enough Builders in your life. If not, please find some. They will build you up, and then you also can Build Up others in your world.

We all flourish when we practice *The Art of Building Up*.

So let's encourage each other and build each other up.[26]

A COMMITMENT TO GROWING AS A BUILDER

I am sure that you, like me, want to become more Builder than Boring or Breaker. The process of growth and change always starts with self-awareness of our current disposition and a vision of what we could be and want to be. Once we recognise how we act more like Breakers or the Boring in certain situations, we can decide that we want to grow as Builders in those situations instead. The next challenge is to turn those new intentions into actions.

So in closing this chapter, I will leave you with ten practical things you can do to practice and grow in *The Art of Building Up*.

Consider ticking off those actions that you already do, and putting a cross next to the ones that you know you need to develop:

TEN THINGS TO DO TO GROW AS A BUILDER:

☐ Recognise and believe that your life is deeply meaningful to others. Make this your new life decision too, just as I did. Then overflow!

☐ Be more others-focused, and less self-focused. It's not always about you. You get built up as you build others up.

☐ Smile more! At everyone. Even random people. At the check-out. Joy makes a massive impact on any relational environment. A smile breaks Boring every time.

☐ Ask *"how are you?"* more often. And mean it. Be more interested in others.

☐ Be more curious, less judgmental, and presumptuous. Ask more questions. Talk less about yourself, and only when others inquire.

☐ Practice saying something positive and encouraging to everyone you meet. Whenever you think something good about someone, make a point of sharing it with them. Say it or send them a quick message. Why would you hold that back?

☐ Today, be intentional to interact with at least three strangers by saying something like *"Hi, have a great day!"* to them. And say it with a smile!

☐ Give to others what you want to receive for yourself. Be the first, even if you don't first receive anything.

☐ Do random acts of kindness. Not just to those who you know and who can repay you. Experience the joy of giving without expecting anything in return.

☐ When you have reason to be a Breaker, stop. Take the higher ground. Forgive. Give a second and third and 70x70 chance. (We'll learn more about how to do this well in *The Art of Forgiving Well*).

Let's be Builders, not Breakers.

And definitely less Boring!

Because love builds up.

In the next chapter, we will go a little deeper to understand why we act and react like we do, as we learn *The Art of Feeling Well*.

Pause to think and talk about The Art of Building Up:

⇒ What is the one thing that you found most relevant or helpful in this chapter?

⇒ Now that you have read the whole chapter, revisit the self-awareness questions posted earlier:

o *Do you think that your friends/family/colleagues would generally describe you to be more of a Breaker, a Builder or Boring?*

o *What effect do you have on your relational environments? Do you generally act and react more thermometer-like, or thermostat-like?*

o Or think of it this way: *What happens when you walk into a room? Do you tend to have a positive, neutral or negative impact on the relational environments that you step into?*

⇒ In response to the truth in this chapter, what is the one thing you can do differently in order to grow in Loving Well?

The Art of Feeling Well

Because what is in you
will affect what comes out of you

The *Art of Feeling Well* will give you the ability to understand and manage your emotions in a positive way for the sake of healthy relationships.

The reason why this is so important is that any change we seek externally usually starts right on the inside of us. Relational climate change begins right in your own heart.

The mouth speaks what the heart is full of.[27]

Above all else, guard your heart, for everything you do flows from it.[28]

What's in our heart will come out of our mouth and will have a significant influence on our relational climate, for good or for bad. And in case we think taping our mouths shut might stop that from happening, what's going on inside us always overflows in all sorts of actions, reactions and non-actions, and our attitudes towards things and people.

By "Feeling Well" I mean being in a state where you are deeply aware of what is going on inside you emotionally. It's about tuning in to your true feelings and understanding how these affect your behaviours in various relational situations.

Hurt in you will hurt those around you.

Hope in you spreads hope to those around you.

The love in you will change the relational climate around you.

One new decision I made in my own journey to Feeling Well is that *I will feel all my feelings fully and discharge them safely and completely.* [31] No more stuffing feelings down like I used to do, allowing them to subconsciously govern my actions and reactions.

Think about that phrase I used: *"Discharge them safely and completely."* Many of us are not very good at this and need a lot of help. I certainly did. Step one to grow in this is to get more in touch with our feelings and *why* we have certain strong emotions. The next step then is to improve our skills to express and communicate these feelings well. That's what *The Art of Speaking Well*, *The Art of Engaging Well*, and *The Art of Fighting Well*, will help us with in the chapters following.

STUFFERS AND PUFFERS

I like to say that when it comes to dealing with what's going on inside us, some are "Stuffers" and others are "Puffers". All of us fall somewhere on this Puffer-Stuffer spectrum:

Stuffers

Stuffers don't like to wear their emotions on their sleeve. They try to suppress and control their true feelings, so that on the surface it looks like all is calm. But what's inside always comes out in some way, doesn't it? Anyone who has been on the receiving end of passive aggressive behaviour understands that while some people may not wear their negative emotions on their sleeve, they sure know how to give you the cold shoulder! They say all is ok when it's obviously not. Rather than saying what needs to be said, they try to send a message of their disapproval and disappointment by withholding words and actions. Or they use apparently friendly language to thinly disguise those things.

Puffers

Puffers, on the other hand, have very little control over their emotions. Like an active volcano, dangerous and destructive spurts of emotions can erupt at any time, and for any reason. Puffers put everyone in their relational environments on constant high alert because no one ever knows what big or small thing will set them off, or when. They are characterised by overreactions, habitually using harsh words, outbursts, quick mood swings, and physical withdrawal to make their disappointment and disapproval known to everyone. While the Stuffer gives the cold shoulder, the Puffer bangs their first on the table to make sure everyone knows how upset they now are.

Stuffers tend to bring an uncomfortable chill into their relational environments, while Puffers add dark, threatening storm clouds that can burst open at any time. Neither is conducive to a healthy relational climate because both, in their different ways, make it hard for others to feel they can speak freely.

Whether you are more of a Stuffer or a Puffer at the moment, I hope that this Art will help you on your journey to Feeling Well as you *"feel your feelings fully and commit to discharging them safely"*.

FEELING YOUR FEELINGS

Becoming aware of the connection between what is in you and what's coming out of you is a vital part of Loving Well. It may be good to start with a personal evaluation and ask yourself questions like: *Does what is in me often come out of me in an unhealthy and unhelpful way?*

Or you may be honest enough to consider whether any of the following are true for you:

- ☐ Your emotional responses are disproportionate to the given situation. You fly off the handle over the smallest things.
- ☐ There are several big things going on in your life that you have never talked to anyone else about.

☐ You find it difficult to celebrate someone else's success. Or, someone else's success makes you feel like a failure.

☐ You experience *schadenfreude* (a German saying, meaning pleasure derived by someone from another person's misfortune)

☐ You feel nothing when you hear of other people's misfortunes.

☐ You often find yourself saying things that you do not mean.

☐ You have very little grace for others' mistakes.

☐ Your mind is constantly occupied with negative thoughts about yourself or others.

Having a healthy self-awareness means knowing your strengths, weaknesses, values, personality, beliefs, motivations, biases, preferences, and default reactions.

Remember when I said earlier that the biggest room in the world is the room for improvement, and that this room is often right in our own house? Well, in this case this is excellent news to understand, because this is the one place where we all have great deal of personal influence and control. I can do something to change myself, even if I cannot do anything to change others in my relational environment.

I can be the change I want to see.

The first step to doing anything about climate change is to assess what the current climate is accurately. Once you have an accurate reading, you can make an appropriate adjustment. This is our first task, so let's take a journey into your inner world - your "iceberg."

ICEBERGS

Whenever there is talk about Global Warming, there is invariably a reference to icebergs and how their changing state is a key indicator of the problem. The iceberg is also a good illustration of how our internal life affects our relational climate. We all have our own "iceberg", made up of 10% that is visible and experienced by others, and then there's the mass of emotions, decisions, hopes, fears, and values that make up what lies beneath the surface. What is below the water determines what is seen above the waterline. The hidden things in our hearts have a significant influence on us, so the more conscious we can become of our inner world, the more effectively we can engage with our outer world.

> The more conscious we are of our inner world, the more effectively we can engage with our outer world.

Until just a few years ago, I was very unaware of my "iceberg". I often joked that I was not very deep emotionally, and when conversations began heading towards the deeper end, I would check out or try to lighten the moment. I just didn't want to and wasn't comfortable with going there. I really was not good at doing deep.

On my journey of trying to grow in this important area I attended an *Emotionally Healthy Leadership* seminar presented by Pete and Geri Scazzero[29]. Here's how I heard them describe the practice of "Exploring Your Iceberg":

> To 'explore the iceberg' is to look beneath the surface of our lives, identifying the hidden but powerful forces that shape the way we navigate choices and relationships. By acknowledging and naming these realities, we raise our emotional awareness, which in turn enables us to process our emotions in a healthier way and to integrate them into our discernment of God's will.

I'm going to give you my own version of how you can start to explore your iceberg but let me first tell you that doing this has been a significant part in my own journey to Feeling Well. As I worked through this exercise it was as if the lights started coming on for me. The questions helped me to focus on my real feelings, and then to give words to articulate these feelings. I began to identify and then express my true feelings in a few key areas, and a process began for me that has been tremendously healing and freeing, and I can honestly say that I now *Feel Well* as a result. It sure took a good dose of vulnerability, honesty, and digging as deep as I could, but the results have been so worth it as I am now much more aware of the connection between my inner and outer life.

HOW TO EXPLORE YOUR ICEBERG

From what I've learnt, read, and practised, I have developed my own version of exploring the iceberg to help you Feel Well: It's a simple set of questions that you can either answer on your own by writing down your responses, or better still, writing down your answers and then discussing each of them with a close friend or confidant.

Note that the objective at this stage is not to "fix" you, but simply to "feel". It's about an honest examination of our feelings and emotions and learning to articulate them well, both for our own sake and the sake of others who are trying to get along with us. Also, it is not about being self-absorbed (it's all about me), nor about being self-conscious (focused on what others think of me).

Remember: *You are only as strong as you are honest.*

And again: *Faith can't fix what you won't face.*

So let's do the iceberg exercise:
Prepare by slowing down. Sit. Get a cup of tea.

Turn your phone off. Close the laptop.

Slow down your breathing.

Have some paper or a journal ready for writing down your insights and responses.

Get into a safe place alone, or with someone you trust and with whom you can be completely honest.

Ask God to help you. Invite him into your inner world and give him full access. Remember, he is also very interested in what is going on inside of you:

> *Behold, you desire truth in the innermost being, and in the hidden part of my heart you will make me know wisdom.*[30]

Now, take some time to answer these questions below. I find that it's best to write your responses down, rather than just thinking about them. There's something powerful and real about putting my responses down on paper.

> Remember:
> You are only
> as strong as
> you are honest.

Question 1: What are you anxious, worried or concerned about right now?

(Prompts: Your health, finances, relationships, job. What do you fear? What keeps you awake at night?)

Question 2: What are you hurt or disappointed about?

(Prompts: Who did something to you? What has not worked out? What's gone wrong?)

Question 3: What are you angry, upset or sad about?

(Prompts: What have you lost? What brings up negative emotions when you think about it? Who are you angry with?)

Question 4: What are you happy and thankful about?
(Prompts: What has gone well? What brings you joy? What have you got? Who has been good to you?)

Question 5: What is my body saying to me?
(Prompts: Am I sleeping well? Low energy? Am I experiencing unusual pain? Is my weight going drastically up or down?)

Question 6: Who or what has shaped me? Who or what is shaping me now?
(Prompts: Where did I learn to behave or react? How is my past experience influencing my present behaviour or reactions?)

Extra question for emoji users: Which emoji/s would you use to describe how you are feeling about your life now? Or draw your own.

Pause for a brief evaluation:

1. How was that exercise for you?
   - ⇒ Easy
   - ⇒ Ok
   - ⇒ Difficult

2. How would you rate yourself on a scale of 1 - 7 on "Being comfortable and able to express your feelings fully"?

   1   2   3   4   5   6   7

3. Can you see any way in which any of these feelings are leaking out of you through words, attitudes, actions or reactions, and how this is negatively affecting your relationships? Try to describe this.

4. A helpful addition to explore your iceberg a little deeper is to ask the "why" question about these emotions:

   - ⇒ *Why am I so angry? Touchy? Judgmental? Defensive?*
   - ⇒ *Why am I so easily offended by* _____*?*
   - ⇒ *Why was I so irritated by what happened or what they said?*
   - ⇒ *Why do I fear* _____ *so much?*
   - ⇒ *Why do I always clam up in those situations?*
   - ⇒ *Why can't I bring myself to speak to* _____ *about* _____*?*

Remember that this exercise is not about "fixing" you, but simply to help you to start feeling your feelings more fully.

INNER HEALING

While the focus of Feeling Well is more on awareness than on healing, I want to close this chapter with a few important thoughts on what you can do to find healing for some of the painful and upsetting emotions that may have surfaced through exploring your iceberg.

Facing your real feelings will not always be comfortable; it sure wasn't for me! It may even result in you becoming aware of yet deeper turmoil in your soul that until then had lain buried beneath the surface. Realising and facing the connection between your inner and outer world may result in some new feelings of anxiety or even fear.

Let's be real about this: Emotional pain, anxiety, depression, being broken-hearted, weary of soul, or having a wounded spirit, are as real as any physical pain and disease, and these are often the terrible consequences of *The Global Cooling Problem*. The journey to inner health and Feeling Well will at times be painful, but always be worth it, for your benefit, and the benefit of those in your relational environments. Here are some closing thoughts to this chapter about what you can do to find healing for negative emotions:

Sound counselling

Firstly, I am all in support of sound counselling, and even taking the appropriate medication where necessary. I would, however, warn readers to wisely evaluate who counsels you, and to be very wary of becoming reliant on medication.

The Great Counsellor and Healer

I am also convinced that there is a Great Counsellor, your Maker, who is the Healer of the broken-hearted,[32] and the Prince of Peace.[33] The meaning of the word *peace* in Biblical Hebrew is "to be complete and whole". Literally, "to live well". In the New Testament, the word peace refers to "God's gift of wholeness", speaking of "when all essential parts are joined together."[34]

I am convinced that every person, no matter what their external circumstances, can fully experience this incredible inner wholeness through Jesus Christ.

He heals the broken-hearted and binds up their wounds.[35]

In his letter to the Philippians, the Apostle Paul gives a helpful prescription by which you can begin your journey to healing from the inside out by coming to God with your feelings:

Don't fret or worry. Instead of worrying, pray. Let petitions and praises shape your worries into prayers, letting God know your concerns. Before you know it, a sense of God's wholeness, everything coming together for good, will come and settle you down. ***It's wonderful what happens when Christ displaces worry at the centre of your life.****[36]*

Let's read that last sentence again: *It's wonderful what happens when Christ displaces worry at the centre of your life.*

That is a beautiful picture and promise! His peace can displace your worry about your problems. He has an answer for your anxieties.

A more regular translation of that promise is: *And the peace of God, which passes all understanding, will guard your heart and mind in Christ Jesus.* [37]

This is what love does: It makes whole. It brings the pieces together. It heals us from the inside out. And this is my prayer for you: that you would experience this fully in your life.

Perhaps pause for a moment and invite God the Healer and Peace-Giver to the secret and deepest places of your heart with the words of this prayer of David from Psalm 139:

> *Search me, O God, and know my heart*
> *test me and know my anxious thoughts.*
> *Point out anything in me that offends you,*
> *and lead me along the path of everlasting life.*

You can find God's peace. You can Feel Well.

And when you Feel Well, you can Love Well.

Let's grow in doing that well.

Pause to think and talk about The Art of Feeling Well:

⇒ What is the one thing that you found most relevant or helpful in this chapter?

⇒ Consider which of the iceberg exercise questions you most struggle to express with words to others?

⇒ Looking again at Philippians 4:6-7 quoted at the end of this chapter, take a moment to bring a current personal worry or concern to God in prayer right now. Be still for a while and let a specific promise from the Scriptures come to your memory to build your faith and peace.

⇒ In response to the truth in this chapter, what is the one thing you can do differently to grow in Loving Well?

The Art of Listening Well

Because to be listened to is to be loved

I n the previous chapter, we looked at *The Art of Feeling Well*, which is all about being self-aware for the sake of healthy relationships. In this chapter, *The Art of Listening Well* is about becoming more others-aware for the purpose of flourishing relationships.

Without Listening Well, we will not be able to Love Well.

Did you hear about the man who asked a pastor to pray for his hearing? Super keen, the pastor immediately began a fervent prayer for the man to be able to hear clearly again, and then, making a sound, asked: *"Is your hearing any better now?"* A little bemused, the man replied: *"My hearing is only due in court on Wednesday morning, pastor!"*

Or the young girl who said to her distracted father: *"Daddy, please will you listen to me read?"* *"Yes, I am listening,"* said the dad, slightly impatiently. *"Silly daddy,"* she replied. *"Don't you know you have to listen with your eyes as well?"*

Or the wife who complains to her husband: *"You don't talk to me anymore,"* and he replies: *"You don't listen to me anymore."*

We will rarely have a healthy relational climate when we are not practising *The Art of Listening Well*. Listening Well is a significant relational climate change agent, and those who Listen Well will certainly cause love to flourish.

> Being heard is so close to being loved that for the average person they are almost indistinguishable.[38]

To be listened to is to be loved.

That's a powerful truth.

Like with Loving Well, the evaluation of whether you Listen Well is not based on whether *you* felt like you did it well, but whether the other person felt heard and understood by you.

And by whether you *really* listened and understood them.

The Art of Listening Well requires heart and skill: a heart that is genuinely interested in others and the skill that enables you to truly get into the other person's shoes so that they "feel felt" and understood. Real listening isn't just about hearing the facts, but also the feelings.

Learning to Listen Well is an absolutely vital part of Loving Well. It will make a profound difference in any conversation and, therefore, in any relationship. Any growth we can do in this vital skill will pay huge dividends in all areas of our lives.

The Quaker author Douglas Steere describes what happens when we Listen Well:

> *To listen to another's soul... may well be almost the greatest service that any human being ever performs for another.*[39]

To listen is to serve, and as Jesus said, the greatest amongst us is the one who serves.[40] In fact, Jesus is an excellent example of a good listener. He left his world to enter ours, putting himself in our shoes to empathise. Although known for his incredible teaching, Jesus is also famous for all the questions he asked those who came to him, including even those who challenged and accused him. His questions always bring the real issues to light, drawing everyone who listens closer to the truth that can set them free.

To Listen Well invites others into your world. It puts aside one's own agenda and says to others: *"I'm interested in you."*

I recently had a special experience with a homeless guy in London that reminded me of what happens when we Listen Well. I'd been reading Bob Goff's book, *Love Does*, and had been challenged to try to live out his call to *"love everyone always"*. I'd decided to start carrying some cash notes with me to give away randomly as I came across needs. That sounds virtuous, but the morning after saying, *"Yes, I'll try to love everyone always"*, it was raining (for a change) in London, and I was running late to the office. As I jumped off the bus, I saw a homeless guy sitting in the rain. Of course, I ran past him... but as I did my freshly made intention sounded an alarm in my conscience. I stopped and turned back to him. We had a good chat in the rain while loads of people walking by. I ended up giving him £15 to get into a hostel for that night, and off I went to work.

The next week I saw the same guy again, this time on my way home. As he saw me, his first words to me were: *"Hi Wolfgang!"* Out of all the people interacting with him, he remembered my name! I replied: *"Hi Errol."* I remembered his name! We both felt special. We'd listened to each other well when we'd met the week before. Everyone has a name, and everyone has a story. Everyone is special and uniquely created in God's glorious image. When we understand each other's longings, loves, losses, hopes, and fears, it humanises us. Something special happens between people when we Listen Well.

Of course, I have also failed the Listening Well test many, many times. I distinctly remember a moment some years ago in the foyer of the venue where we were meeting as a church. I was speaking to someone, and a few minutes into our conversation, she paused and said to me: "Wolfi, when I am talking to you, it often feels like you are looking over my shoulder, *scanning the room to see who you need to speak to next."* Ouch!

That shocked me, and since that day I have been trying my very best to give the person I am talking to my full attention. I hope you'll experience this from me when next we're speaking!

BEING QUICK TO LISTEN

The Apostle James instructs us as follows: *My dear brothers and sisters, take note of this: Everyone should be quick to listen, slow to speak and slow to become angry.* [41]

Note a few key words/phrases from this instruction:

It's for "Everyone"

This is for every one of us. We are never excused from Listening Well because of our specific temperament or issues. Don't use your impatience or busyness as an excuse. Practise *The Art of Growing Up* and become the better listener that everyone around you longs for you to be.

We should be "slow to become angry"

This relates to *The Art of Feeling Well, which we examined in the previous chapter. "Slow" here calls for us to express our feelings safely and truthfully to create a healthy relational climate. Note that it doesn't say, "Never become angry." Many things should provoke* righteous anger in us, but our response should be purposefully measured to bring about true change, not just to blow off some emotional steam.

We should be "slow to speak"

We will look at the heart and skill of this in *The Art of Speaking Well*, but for now, let's just note that God gave us one mouth, but two ears, so let's start by trying to listen twice as much as we speak. Make sure that you truly understand before you reply. Consider that "listen" and "silent" are spelt with the same letters.

We should be "quick to listen"

This means that Listening Well is our default position towards others. Those around us should not need to beg or ask or nag us to Listen Well. We often compliment speakers on speaking well. How about becoming those who will be complimented because we Listen Well.

But listening doesn't just require our ears. Remember what the little girl replied to her distracted father? *"Silly daddy! Don't you know you have to listen with your eyes as well?"*

Consider these lists of ten practical Dos and Don'ts that will help you to Listen Well:

Here are ten Dos to help you to Listen Well:

1. Do be fully present, focussing fully on the person in order to tune in to the non-verbal cues that are part of what they are trying to share with you.

2. Do intentionally take the focus off yourself by quieting your mind from your own agenda to be fully engaged and to hear at heart level with empathy and real understanding.

3. Do give the speaker your full attention by removing all distractions as per Don't number 1 above. This is worth repeating here because it is a real culprit in our overconnected and super-distracted culture.

4. Do set your objective to understand fully, not just to give your reply, defence, or opinion. Once the speaker feels more fully understood by you, perhaps they will be more open to understanding what you have to say.

    Seek first to understand, before seeking to be understood. [42]

5. Do listen for feeling words, not just fact words. For example, when someone tells you that *"you always/never do that"*, don't correct them on the facts. Rather hear what they are feeling.

6. Do suspend any judgment of motives or actions. Judgment will always cloud what you hear. Be willing to listen without judgment. Live interested in others. Be curious about their *why*. Listening builds trust – we don't trust people who don't understand who we are.

7. Do practise "reflective listening", which is simply trying to repeat back to the speaker as accurately as you can what you think you heard them say, and then to ask: *Is that correct?* Do ask clarifying questions, if necessary, like: *Can you just explain that part to me?* or *How did that make you feel?*

8. Do watch your body language. Folded hands, no eye contact, and turning sideways all communicate a measure of resistance or disinterest in what is being said.

9. When someone seems to be struggling to fully express what they want to say to you, help them by asking: *Is there anything else you would like to add?*

10. Do clarify what is most important to the speaker by asking at the end of a conversation: *Of everything you have shared what is the most important thing you want me to remember?*

Here are ten Don'ts that will help you to Listen Well:

1. Don't be distracted by your phone, laptop, watch, or other people passing by. Put the phone down, preferably out of sight. Close the laptop. Pause the TV, or better still, switch it off. Also, please turn off those sound and vibrating notifications on your devices - do you really need to know each time someone likes your social media post?

2. Don't listen to reply, but to understand.

3. Don't assume that you know why someone is asking you a difficult/tricky question. Before you rush into answering, simply clarify by asking: *Why do you ask that question?*

4. Don't interrupt the speaker by interpreting, advising, or correcting.

5. Don't finish sentences or stories for the speaker.

6. Don't respond by trying to trump their story with something similar that's happened to you. (Like saying, *That's nothing, you should have seen when I...*)

7. Don't give your opinion or answer before you fully understand the question.

8. Don't focus on trying to fix the problem, but rather on trying to understand the problem, and empathise.

9. Don't confuse listening with agreement. To listen to someone does not mean that you agree with them. It's not a compromise to listen to really understand another's opinion or view.

10. Don't be afraid of some silence. You don't need to fill every pause in a conversation with words.

And here are ten tips for the speaker:

Of course, communication takes at least two people listening and speaking to each other. If we are the speaker, we should also commit ourselves to making it as easy as possible for the listener to understand what we are trying to communicate. Consider these ten tips for the speaker to improve being heard and understood:

1. Think before you speak. Separate facts and feelings. What exactly is it you want communicated, or understood?

2. Be honest, clear, direct, and respectful. Say what you really mean. Be truthful. (Use *The Art of Engaging Well*)

3. Get to the point as quickly as possible. Don't beat around the bush. If you want something, ask for it. If you want someone to do something, say exactly what you want done. Keep it as concise as possible. Don't waste words.

Confusion grows in direct proportion to the number of words used. Speak plainly and briefly, using the shortest, most familiar words.

4. Speak in the "I". Own what you say. Personalise (*"I often..."*), don't generalise (*We always... or One always...*).

5. Be authentic. The real you is the best you.

6. Own your feelings. Don't blame others for the way you feel. Instead of saying: *You make me feel dishonoured*, rather say: *When you do _____, I feel dishonoured.*

7. Make sure your tone of voice matches what you are trying to communicate.

8. Watch your body language. Look the listener in the eye. Have an open posture towards them.

9. Watch your speaking pace. Speak at a natural pace, with appropriate pauses.

10. Give the hearer appropriate opportunity to respond, and to ask clarifying questions.

Most of us can probably admit that we have a lot of growing to do in *The Art of Listening Well*. If it's true that *"Being heard is so close to being loved that for the average person they are almost indistinguishable"*,[43] then it should be clear that growing in this climate-changing Art will have a significant impact on all our relational environments.

To Listen Well is to Love Well.

Let's grow in doing that well.

Pause to think and talk about The Art of Listening Well:

⇒ On a scale of 1 - 7, how would you rate yourself as a good listener?

⇒ On a scale of 1-7, how would your close friends/ spouse/ colleagues rate you as a good listener?

⇒ What is the one thing that you found most relevant or helpful in this chapter?

⇒ Of the practical tips for Listening Well listed toward the end of the chapter, which three do you need to work on the most?

⇒ In response to the truth in this chapter, what is the one thing you can do differently to grow in Loving Well?

The Art of Speaking Well

Because words are powerful climate change agents

Words are one of the most potent relational climate changers. Our words have a massive impact on every area of our lives, and in this chapter, we will look at how to use our words well to positively influence our relational climate so that our relationships can flourish.

You can say that you love someone, but does what you say and how you say it really say *"I love you"* like the one hearing you needs to hear it from you? Do they *feel* loved by what you say and how you say it?

The way we use our words is one of the most evident measures of our maturity.

The great Apostle Paul recognised that his words were a crucial part of his own maturing when he related: *"When I was a child, I spoke as a child, but when I became a man, I put away childish things."*

To Love Well, we need to grow out of childish ways of using words.

To the Ephesian church (and I would suggest that this applies to any group, team, or organisation), Paul said: *"Then we will no longer be immature like children. ... Instead, we will speak the truth in love, growing in every way more and more like Christ."* [44]

Here we see that our growing up, and what we say and how we say it, are strongly linked together. Our words and how we use them can be one of the most potent growth catalysts in any relationship, organisation, church, family, team, or friendship group. You will flourish according to how you use words to set the right relational climate. Conversely, our words can also be the most destructive force in our relationships.

THE POWER OF WORDS

The first thing to know about words is that they are very powerful.

Unfortunately, the old English children's rhyme *"Sticks and stones may break my bones, but words will never harm me"* isn't true, because words can and do hurt if not used well.

As the Proverb says, *"there is life and death in the power of the tongue".*[45]

Our words can bless, build up, and break down.

They can limit or launch others.

Our words can hurt and wind people up. They can encourage and give others hope.

Christians believe that the very world was created and formed when God spoke and declared, *"Let there be",* and that *"all things are upheld by the word of his power."* [46] Jesus cursed an unfruitful fig tree, and it withered. He said to the storm, *"Be still",* and it was. He instructed his followers to speak in order to move mountains.

In the same way, I believe that you and I create and shape the world and environment in which we live by the words we say (and don't say). Our words can grow our world or shrink it.

> Words are powerful, so we must use them wisely carefully and skilfully.

Because words are powerful, to Love Well requires us to grow in using our words wisely, carefully, and skilfully.

It may be helpful to consider what your words have been creating lately? Perhaps you could get a little vulnerable with a friend and ask them what they have been hearing coming out of your mouth?

Have your words revealed you as a Breaker, a Builder, or Boring? Have you started using meaningless words or phrases, like *"Oh my god"*? Some curse words? A constant stream of complaining? Words of faith, or fear? Truth or lies? Double-talk? Gossiping? Thankfulness? Words of encouraging others?

I'm sure that you have seen a word cloud, which is an image made up of the words used in a particular text or speech, in which the size of each word indicates its importance or frequency of use. For example, here's a word cloud of the introduction chapter of this book, inviting you to Love Well:

It would be an interesting exercise to have a word cloud made of our daily conversations, to see which words most frequently come out of our mouths and whether the majority are Builder or Breaker words. It's a good habit to evaluate the words that are coming out of our mouths.

Our words have the power to cause our relationships to wither or to flourish. When you recognise this, you will start to use your words more carefully, and commit to growing in using them well.

We have all said things that we have regretted. Words that have hurt others. Words that have chilled a relational climate like when the sun dips behind a cloud on an autumn day. Words spoken out are like squeezed toothpaste. Try getting that back into the tube!

Jesus had a lot to say about words, including a strong warning about using words carelessly: *"I tell you that every careless word that people speak, they will give an accounting for it in the day of judgment."* [47]

Ouch.

The Wisdom books of the Bible also give us a lot of helpful advice on controlling our tongues, for example:

> *There is a time to be silent and a time to speak.* [48]

> *Set a guard over my mouth, LORD; keep watch over the door of my lips.* [49]

> *Whoever guards his mouth and tongue, keeps his soul from trouble.* [50]

TAMING THE TONGUE

In the Bible, the Apostle James starts his letter in which he is emphasising the importance of faith being lived out, by stressing the importance of controlling the tongue: *"If we could control our tongues, we would be perfect and could also control ourselves in every other way."* [51] Wow, that's quite a challenging statement. Read it again. If we could learn to control the tongue, we could control ourselves in every other way.

He continues to explain that *"We can make a large horse go wherever we want by means of a small bit in its mouth. And a small rudder makes a huge ship turn wherever the pilot chooses to go, even though the winds are strong."* [52]

Then he says that *"no one can tame it".* [53]

You can't *tame* the tongue, but you can *guide* it. The idea of controlling the tongue means to guide, to hold in check, restrain, or to lead by a bridle, like a powerful horse being steered by a small bit in its mouth.

You guide your tongue by guarding your heart. Jesus rightly taught that our mouths speak what our hearts are full of.[54] So the tongue is guided by what is in our hearts. Our tongues are an accurate measure of what is going on in our hearts. When there is love in the heart, words of love will come from the mouth.

A heart of love will guide the mouth to speak the truth in love.

USING THE RIGHT WORDS MAKES ALL THE DIFFERENCE

Words used well are a great blessing to those around us, and the writer of Proverbs is right to observe that *"Everyone enjoys a fitting reply; it is wonderful to say the right thing at the right* time!" [55], and *"Like apples of gold in settings of silver is a word spoken at the right time".* [56]

But there can also be death in the tongue.[57]

In his letter to the Ephesians, the Apostle Paul continues his instruction about a culture of maturing and growing like this:

> *Let no corrupting talk come out of your mouths, but only such as is good for building up, as fits the occasion, that it may give grace to those who hear.*[58]

Corrupting words are words that are rotten, useless, of poor quality, and unfit for use. The same verse in The Message Translation reads: *"Say only what helps, each word a gift."*

Just the idea of a "rotten" word in our mouths should put us off, but it's so easy to fall into a habit of using words poorly so that instead of them being a gift, they are critical, judgmental, limiting, and negative.

How we use words makes a big difference.

SPEAKING THE TRUTH IN LOVE

The Apostle Paul also instructs believers to *"speak the truth in love."* [59] Words are particularly powerful when they are true and are spoken in love.

To Speak Well is always to speak the truth, and to speak it in love. Jesus said, *"My Word is truth"* [60] and that *"the truth will set you free."* [61]

Truth breaks the power of lies that bind and control us.

But all this power is lost if the truth isn't spoken in love.

If I could speak all the languages of earth and of angels, but didn't love others, I would only be a noisy gong or a clanging cymbal. [62]

A word to us Christians about using the Word well

If you consider yourself a Christian, please note that this call to "speak the truth in love" infers that merely quoting a bible verse at someone (or posting it on social media) doesn't mean anything if you don't do it in love. It may be the truth, but when it's not spoken in love, you're not saying anything useful. In fact, possibly the opposite: You're just making an irritating noise and reinforcing the stereotype your friends already have about Christians (and you).

When you speak the truth in love, the Scripture acts like a sharp scalpel penetrating deep into the heart and minds of your hearers (or readers) in a way that leads to life. Without love, the sharp two-edged sword may just wound, or at worse, kill. Remember that the law came through Moses, but grace and truth came through Jesus Christ. [63] It's always grace and truth. Never grace without truth, nor truth without grace. It's never truth or love, but always truth in love.

To the Colossians, the Apostle Paul writes:

Live wisely among those who are not believers and make the most of every opportunity. Let your conversation be gracious and attractive (full of grace, seasoned with salt) so that you will have the right response for everyone.[64]

The truth is made "attractive" when it is "full of grace, seasoned with salt". The analogy here is that when we present Jesus' Word of truth to someone, we season it well with his grace and his love. The law and legalism never season the truth well, but in fact spoil it. Remember that the point of love is relationship, so a measure of whether the truth has been spoken in love is simply: *Has what you have said and the way you have said it moved someone closer to relationship with God or not?*

A word to us preachers about the words we preach

Here's a though for all of us preachers (and to those of you who try to share God's Good News with others): Think about how often you declare to your listeners that "you must" (do this or that), versus a grace-empowered "you can" (Because God did, you can do this and that).

There's a significant nuance to this which I realised after evaluating a message I preached at one of our European Student camps a few years ago. My focus had been to encourage students to stand strong in their faith against all that opposes them in their culture. Upon reflection, I realised that my message had been full of *"to overcome, you must do this... and must do that"* statements. That's all good, but it's not as powerful as declaring that *"because of what God has done in Christ, you CAN overcome".* You *can* do it because he has done it. This is Gospel-centred preaching. The words I used in that message put the emphasis on the hearer's discipline, rather than on God's amazing, empowering grace to every believer. This incident had a significant impact on my preaching since then, and I encourage all my preacher friends to consider what message your words and the way you use them is really sending.

DO NOT LIE

The instruction about speaking truth in love continues like this in the letter to the Ephesians: *"So each of you must get rid of your lying (falsehood). Speak the truth to your neighbour. We are all parts of one body."* [65]

> *Love does not lie.*
>
> *Lying is saying what isn't true.*
>
> *Lying erodes trust.*
>
> *Lies will never improve your relational climate (not even "white lies").*
>
> *Lies always destroy the relational climate.*
>
> *When is the last time you lied?*

Lying includes saying yes when you mean no, or no when you mean yes. Do you do that? Think of how truthfully you answer the following kinds of questions:

⇒ *Did I disappoint you?* "No." (But you told your other friend that you were, in fact, very disappointed not to be invited.)

⇒ *Are you ok?* "Yes." (But you feel upset about it.)

⇒ *Will you come?* "Sure, I'd love to." (But you already have so much on and vowed to be at home that evening.)

⇒ *Does this jacket suit me?* "Yes." (Even though you really don't like it, but just can't bear to say what you really think, so you just let him look weird.)

A TIP: If you are prone to saying *yes* too quickly, here's a simple hack to help you in those awkward situations: Instead of succumbing to the pressure to give an answer right on the spot, learn to reply with a polite *"Let me think about that,* or *Let me check if I can and get back to you"*. This takes away the pressure of needing to say yes or no and gives you time to consider a truthful and appropriate response. (Then you need to do what you said you would do, and not put it off!) This is a really practical application of being *"slow to speak"*.[66]

THE POWER OF "NO"

"No" can be the right word or the wrong word. Or it can depend on how often you use it. Parents, think about how often you say "no", compared to how often you say "yes" to your children. I recall being at a theme park in a long queue snaking up a large staircase to take a rollercoaster ride. Everyone was excited. Behind me was a dad with two young sons. He must have said "no" to his two boys a hundred times as we slowly made our way up a long set of stairs to the top. Not one yes. There wasn't any obvious danger to them, but he was just in a bad mood and had a bad habit. You know what happens when you cry wolf once too often, right? When "no" really needs to mean "no", it will have lost its power.

BEING SLOW TO TYPE

If the Apostle Paul had been writing in our generation, I'm sure he would have also added that we should be *"slow to type the truth in love"*. We all know of people who have got into some serious trouble, or at least some terrible embarrassment, for posting stupid and insensitive posts or comments on social media. Sadly, the finger also types what the heart is full of. Nicky Gumbel, famous for The Alpha Course, has given this helpful guide to T.H.I.N.K. before you post or comment, asking yourself:

T : Is it true?
H : Is it helpful?
I : Is it inspiring?
N : Is it necessary?
K : Is it kind?

These questions will help you to *be slow to type.*

I have long held a practice that I do not respond in writing to any messages (emails/texts/etc.) that express complaints or negative emotions to me. I believe that the best way to respond is to pick up the phone as soon as possible and talk about it with the person directly. (We'll look at how to do that well in *The Art of Engaging Well*.) If I respond in writing, it is only to set up a face-to-face meeting as soon as possible, not to deal with the issue in writing. We have also adopted this as a practice in our staff team, and I can tell you that it really makes a big difference to how we deal with issues that arise.

SPEAKING WORDS OF BLESSING

Another way to Speak Well is to use words to bless others. The word *bless* in the Greek language is *eulogeó* (to "eulogise") and means "to speak well of". Note that it means to *speak* well, not just to *think* well of someone. Why would you think something good or positive about someone, and not say it to them?

In religious terms, to bless someone means to pronounce words over them that invoke divine favour on them. One of the most well-known blessings in Judeo-Christian circles is the one that the High Priest Aaron prayed over God's people in the book of Numbers:

> *The Lord bless you and keep you;*
> *The Lord make His face shine upon you,*
> *And be gracious to you;*
> *The Lord lift up His countenance upon you,*
> *And give you peace.*[67]

The verse following this explains what happens when this blessing is spoken over the people: *So they shall put My name on the children of Israel, and I will bless them.*

This carries the idea that when we bless, we "put God's Name on" someone. We invoke the favour of heaven on the person through our words. As a church leader, I make a habit of ending most of the church services I lead by speaking this blessing or some version of it over the congregation. God's people desire God's blessing. Everyone needs blessing.

This Aaronic blessing is not a magic formula for us today, but it should stir us to speak more blessing over those in our relational environments. Words of affirmation that confirm who people are, instead of who and what they are not. Words that recognise and affirm the image of God in people, rather than their imperfections, sin and brokenness. Words of hope instead of despair and negativity. Words that build confidence and awaken dreams and potential in the other. Words that honour their gifts and talents.

> Why would you think something good or positive about someone, and not say it to them?

Sometimes we may think that we need to hold back with our blessings because the receiver may get a big head. Not too long ago I was intentionally focussing on speaking words of encouragement to someone who was showing some initial signs of improvement after having struggled - even failed - in an area of work. As I did, an observer to this pulled me aside and cautioned me to consider easing back on the praise a little in case the person took it to heart. Well, that's exactly what I wanted for this guy! He needed reminding of who he was, and who he could be. He already knew full well what he wasn't. The world is expert at that, filled with voices telling you that you are not good enough, attractive enough, rich enough, fit enough, successful enough, or cool enough.

We act out of who we think or believe we are, so words that bless speak against this erosive part of our culture and recalibrate us to be who and what we were created to be.

Jesus took the concept of speaking blessing even further when he declared that his followers should *"bless those who curse you."* Wow! Ouch! Why? How?

We can only understand this when we understand that we have been "blessed to be a blessing." God has blessed you, and from the overflow of his blessing you can even bless and speak well of your enemies and those who curse you. Along these same lines, the Apostle Paul instructs the Romans as follows: *"Don't let evil conquer you, but conquer evil by doing good."* [68]

Amazing transformation can happen in the worst of relational climates when we choose this higher way of Speaking Well.

Recall the words I quoted from Martin Luther King's speech earlier in the book where he gives his reason for why he believes Jesus said to love our enemies, which is that *"love has within it a redemptive power. And there is a power there that eventually transforms individuals".*

That's what words of blessing spoken in love do. They transform. They cause blessing - divine favour - to flow from us into our relational environments, and when that takes hold and becomes part of the culture, everyone will begin to flourish. Commit yourself to growing in *The Art of Speaking Well*, and I believe you will begin to see some significant positive relational climate change around you.

Perhaps this simple but profound prayer from the Psalms is the best way to end this chapter as we reflect on how we are doing in this Art:

> *May the words of my mouth and the meditation of my heart be pleasing to you, O Lord, my rock and my redeemer.*[69]

To Speak Well is to Love Well.

Let's grow in doing that well.

Because words are powerful,
to Love Well requires us to grow in using our words
wisely, carefully, and skilfully.

Pause to think and talk about The Art of Speaking Well:

⇒ What is the one thing that you found most relevant or helpful in this chapter?

⇒ Imagine a word cloud being formed of the words and phrases you use regularly, and consider:

- If you could eliminate three words/phrases from your word cloud to improve your relational climate, what would these be?

- What three words or phrases do you think would improve your relational climate if they showed up more prominently on your word cloud?

⇒ In response to the truth in this chapter, what is the one thing you can do differently to grow in Loving Well?

The Art of Engaging Well

*Because unresolved issues pollute
our relational environments*

Pollution is a massive problem in any climate. The worst I've ever seen was when I visited Beijing just before the Olympics in 2008. We could not even see the brand-new so-called Bird's Nest stadium from the road because of the smog, and all our photos of the Great Wall of China show a thick cloud of foul air covering this incredible wonder of the world.

Life cannot flourish in a polluted environment. Nor can relationships. Unresolved issues are like air pollution in a re-lational environment. Knowing how to recognise pollution and how to address it well will result in significant positive relational climate change.

I'm sure we've all had situations where something needed to be addressed with someone or discussed within a team, group, or family, but for some reason, it just didn't happen. Or perhaps you tried to say what you thought or felt, and it came out all wrong, and instead of solving the issue, it ended up worse than before. Or maybe you have been on the receiving end of something similar.

Relational climate pollution occurs whenever conflicts, disagreements, unmet expectations, misunderstandings, assumptions, or disappointments are left to hang in the air, without being effectively cleared away. We wait around hoping that some magic wind would clear the air, but this rarely happens.

Engaging Well is *"speaking the truth in love"* [70] in such a way that clears this kind of pollution from your relational environments. In this chapter, I want to help you understand how to do this well, and learn the skill needed to address these issues in a clear, healthy, and timely manner.

This content lays the groundwork for addressing what I will define as "general pollution" issues in our relationships. I truly believe that learning this Art will help you speak to just about anyone about just about any issue that is polluting a relational climate you are in. Of course, there will also be times of higher conflict and sharper disagreements, when you will need not only to Engage Well, but also to Fight Well. That's what the next chapter will deal with, but don't simply jump ahead to that, because if you don't first master *The Art of Engaging Well*, you are probably not going to Fight Well either.

HAVING CRUCIAL CONVERSATIONS

In the New York Times bestseller *Crucial Conversations*, Joseph Grenny, a leading social scientist, gives a compelling reason why *The Art of Engaging Well* is so important. He asserts that *"The health of a relationship, team or organisation is best measured by the average time lag between identifying and discussing problems."* [71]

Notice that he emphasises both the *when* and the *how* aspect of dealing with relational problems. Sadly, our efforts to engage in such scenarios often blow things up rather than grow things up.

> The health of a relationship, team or organisation is best measured by the average time lag between identifying and discussing problems. [71]

We know that how you say something is as important as what you say, as the wisdom of Proverbs reminds us that:

> *A gentle answer turns away wrath, but a harsh word stirs up anger.*[72]

For our *Art of Loving Well* purposes, a "crucial conversation" is one you need to have to address an issue with someone to get yourself, them and your relationship unstuck and to move on to the next level of maturity. I call this "engaging" because it is about intentionally moving into action to address issues with clarity and confidence.

The opposite would be "disengaging", which, interestingly, when used in a military sense, means to withdraw from an area of conflict. Isn't that exactly what we often do when we face relational issues like those mentioned above? In fact, according to Grenny's assertion, the longer we wait to have such conversations to address the issue at hand the less healthy our relationships/teams/organisations/churches are deemed to be.

Engaging Well, on the other hand, will pay huge dividends, including:

1. Helping to surface issues that are eroding trust, unity, or productivity in any relational environment.

2. Getting your relationship, team, or group unstuck from unresolved issues to move forward into a new level of trust and productivity.

3. Helping you place a higher value on the relationships at stake.

Here are some example situations that this Art helps with, when you need to engage in a relationally healthy way to address an issue:

⇒ Your colleague did not do what you had agreed on in the meeting.

⇒ A team member regularly arrives late for meetings.

⇒ Your housemate, child or spouse is not doing their agreed chores.

⇒ A colleague or friend makes a racist or sexist remark during a conversation.

⇒ A team leader corrects you angrily in front of the whole team.

⇒ A friend does not return your call or message as promised.

⇒ Your parents have an unrealistic expectation of you about something.

⇒ Your boyfriend/girlfriend keeps pushing to go beyond the physical affection boundaries you agreed on.

⇒ A person you are trying to help habitually cancels meetings at the last minute.

⇒ Your partner spends more than you budgeted.

⇒ Your employer has not initiated a salary review with you in the past three years. (This was a real situation with a friend, and when he told me he was thinking of quitting because of this, I challenged him to first use this Engage Well skill before making his final decision. I'll let you know what happened to him at the end of this chapter.)

I'm sure you can relate to many of these scenarios and could add quite a few more to this list. You'll agree that all these are tricky and there is no guarantee of them being resolved without a few sparks flying. The question is: How would you engage in these situations?

One other example that intrigues me is the instruction that the Apostle Paul gave to the young leader Timothy when he wrote: *"Command certain people not to teach false doctrines any longer or to devote themselves to myths and endless genealogies"*.[73]

Try to imagine how Timothy would actually go about doing that without losing these people or dividing the church? How would he approach them? What would he say? (Anyone want to be a pastor?!)

It's evident that there is a big gap between receiving an instruction like that, and how one would actually approach such a situation in a way that would bring about a good result. Joseph Grenny also asserts that:

> *"There are moments of disproportionate influence in your life and your leadership: moments where how you and I behave matters more than anything else to the health of our relationships /family/team/church/organisation."* [74]

This means that learning to Engage Well can turn a potentially disengaging relational situation into an opportunity to strengthen and deepen the relationship. Surely that's a good reason to master this Art!

When growing in an art, it's often good or even necessary to stand on the shoulders of giants, and the approach that I propose was significantly shaped by two particular giants, Joseph Grenny[75], and the Scazzeros[76]. From their material and others', I've concluded a strategic four-step process for Engaging Well. I am confident that if you apply these four steps to wherever a crucial conversation is needed, you will get better results than ever before.

Remember: A "skill" is the learned ability to do something well to achieve a predetermined result. We develop skills by being instructed, by learning, practising, repeating, and perfecting. Those who develop skills have better outcomes than those who don't.

THE FOUR STEP PROCESS TO ENGAGING WELL:

1. Create Safety

2. Engage with the Facts

3. Express Preferences or Expectations

4. Negotiate Agreement

To help explain the process, I will describe a simple scenario for us to work through:

You lead a team that serves every third Saturday evening at a charity event. Dave, a previously loyal and punctual team member, has been coming late for the past three times when he has been on duty with you. This has put pressure on you and the other team members, and you have been getting increasingly irritated by this change in behaviour. Although he has offered an apology every time, he hasn't communicated any reason for his lateness with you.

This isn't a critical situation, but quite typical of the kinds of things that crop up to create tension in our relationships. Small things can so quickly become big things if we don't Engage Well.

So here's how we would use the four-step process in this scenario:

First: CREATE SAFETY

Creating safety is about first expressing value for the relationship that is at stake because of the issue that has arisen. We tend to rush to address the issue, but this is a grave error and will significantly reduce the chances of a successful outcome. Instead, always start the conversation by finding as much common ground as you possibly can.

You may begin by saying something like: *"You know, Dave, we've been working together on this team for three great years now. I really appreciate and am thankful for how you have sacrificed to be a part of this. I'm really excited about our future."*

What this does is express mutual respect and purpose. It also communicates a hope for a shared future.

Other helpful phrases could include:

⇒ *I know that you and I both value this ....*
⇒ *You know that I care about you.*
⇒ *I appreciate you...*
⇒ *I am really thankful for you ...*

⇒ *I am committed to working through this for the sake of our relationship and shared future.*

⇒ *I see you as a very valuable part of our team/group.*

⇒ *I love you.* (Maybe don't use this with a colleague!)

If there is anything that you need to apologise for or take ownership of regarding what happened, this is an excellent moment to do so right at the start of the conversation. This creates an atmosphere of humility which will significantly enhance the prospect of gaining agreement later on. There is always some part of the problem to own and thinking you're not any part of the problem is often the problem.

Focussing on creating safety first communicates that you value the relationship, and places this above the issue. Failure to express adequate value for the relationship on the other hand is virtually a guarantee that this conversation will not have a positive outcome.

For example, a while back I received an email from someone about a leader whom we both knew. He listed a number of complaints and accusations against this leader and asked me to mediate between them. There was no humility from his side, only a desire to have his case heard, and to be justified. I replied that since I did not see any expression on his side of desiring reconciliation with this leader, and as such I did not see any hope for a resolution.

Your chance of resolution is directly related to your desire for the restoration of the relationship.

If you don't create safety, there is little hope of a good resolution. However, if you create safety well, you can potentially speak to just about anyone about just about anything.

> If you create safety well, you can potentially speak to just about anyone about just about anything.

Another part of creating safety is choosing the right time and location to meet and speak. This should be appropriate to the intensity of the conversation. Late at night may be good for night owls, but terrible for those who head to bed early. Just before an important event may also not be ideal, unless the issue is relevant to the agenda. Sometimes a public setting may be a good place because we tend to keep our emotions and voices more controlled when there are others around us, but at other times this may restrict openness for the very same reason.

I find the best approach to choosing a setting and time is to suggest one, and then ask the other person whether this is suitable for them. I would also caution against a one-on-one guy and girl conversation, except perhaps in a very public space. In our London staff environment, we have a policy that one-on-one male and female meetings should never take place behind closed doors. If there is a need for such a meeting, which is often the case, we do this in a public space, with the door open, or in a room with a glass door. Whether we like it or not, this is simply wisdom in an age when false perceptions or accusations can so easily ruin reputations even with the very best of intentions.

OK, now it's time to raise the issue.

Second: Engage with the FACTS

This step is about bringing the real issue to the surface as clearly, accurately, and respectfully as possible. Facts are the truth, and if they are clear, they will be indisputable. As Jesus promised: *"...the truth will set you free."* [77] If you embellish or exaggerate the facts, you are no longer speaking the truth.

The misstep here is that instead of engaging with the facts, we often do so with our assumptions, judgments, or with how we feel about the issue. We tend to make up a story about why the person did or did not do the thing. We assume that their motive is bad. As a result, we engage with unhelpful statements such as:

⇒ *Dave, you're always late!*

- This is an exaggeration that is mostly not true. Words like "always" and "never" are feeling words, not fact words, and are rarely helpful to Engaging Well.

⇒ *Dave, you obviously no longer want to be on the team.*

- This is an assumption or judgment you are making. How do you know that he does not want to be on the team?

⇒ *Dave, I feel that you do not respect my leadership.*

- This is you personalising it and making it about you. Never make it about you, until you are very clear that it is about you, which it sometimes may well be. But lead the conversation with the facts, not your feelings.

⇒ *Dave, you make me angry!*

- This is not taking ownership of your feelings. You are angry because of what Dave did. So tell him what he did, rather than telling him your feelings about what he did. To own and express your feelings well, say something like: *Dave, when you did* _____ _____, *I felt very disappointed.*

Other unhelpful phrases to avoid are:

⇒ *You don't care.*
⇒ *You never help me.*
⇒ *You always let me down.*
⇒ *You are always late.*
⇒ *You always only think of yourself.*
⇒ *You never do what we agreed.*
⇒ *You are a real so-and-so.*

You must resist these kinds of statements at all cost, because they are sure to get in the way of a good outcome. Although these may reflect what you feel, they are not the facts, and they will not lead the conversation towards resolution. In fact, if you lead with your feelings about an issue, the focus will very likely end up on you and your feelings, rather than on the other person's actions that need addressing.

Ideally, use "fresh facts"

In a case where much time has passed since something happened that you have been waiting to address, especially when it's about a bad habit or attitude, I recommend that you wait for a "fresh fact" when such behaviour is repeated. Use this to Engage Well, rather than trying to get a person to remember something they have possibly long forgotten.

A TIP: When I am preparing to engage in such a conversation, I find it useful to write the facts down just as above. This helps me to sift through the muddied waters created by any swirling emotions, and state only what I know, versus what I assume or feel. (We'll deal with the feelings part of this in the next chapter on *The Art of Fighting Well*.)

So let's write down the indisputable facts in Dave's case:

1. He has been faithful. (Add: For how long?)
2. He has been late three times. (Add: Exactly how late?)
3. His lateness is negatively affecting team performance. (Add: In what way?)

Based on these facts, your conversation would go something like this: *Dave, I have noticed you have been fifteen minutes late for each of the last three times that we were on duty together as a team.*

There are some key phrases that are helpful to practise to present facts in a non-threatening way:

⇒ *I have noticed that ... (add the facts)*

- This phrase is effective because it simply states an observation of the facts, without judgement or assumption.

⇒ *I am puzzled by ... (add the facts)*

- This is particularly helpful in cases where you previously agreed on something, and it was not done.

⇒ *I'm curious to understand why you ...*

- This is a safe way of asking someone to explain an action or omission.

⇒ *Can I check an assumption I have with you?*

- Say what you are feeling or thinking and give them permission to correct you if necessary.

Once you have stated the facts, you want to give Dave an opportunity to respond, so you simply ask: *"Tell me about that"*, or *"Can you please help me to understand why this is?"*

This is SO important because at this stage there is at least one fact that you do not know: *Why has he started arriving late?*

Always be curious about their why
Never assume that you know this. There could be all sorts of reasons for his lateness and asking this clarifying question will prevent you from making incorrect assumptions and unfair judgments about their actions or motives. It could also

potentially save you a lot of embarrassment. For example, Amanda, one of our London pastors, tells the story of how she was preparing dinner and had expected her husband Dan to be home at an agreed time. He never arrived on time, and the meal got cold, and she got heated, making up all kinds of stories about how Dan didn't care and value her slaving away in the kitchen. When she finally heard him coming in, she was ready to give him a piece of her mind, minus a cold dinner. But she quickly found out that Dan had had an accident on his bike on his way home... oops!

Never assume. Always focus on the facts only and be curious about the why.

Consider a few different answers you could get from Dave about his coming late:

⇒ *You're right. I've had some financial challenges lately and have been too embarrassed to tell anyone. I can't afford to travel by train anymore, so have been trying to get here by bus, but it's not working out as well as I expected.*

- Now you have surfaced something profound. Would you agree that this changes so much of what you were previously thinking? You may also be curious about why Dave did not feel free to tell you of his problem sooner.

⇒ *Well, most of the other guys don't seem to bother to get there on time. Since you never say anything about it, I didn't think it was important to us anymore.*

- Now this is a culture issue, or maybe a personal leadership question about how you are leading the team and how you are setting expectations.

⇒ Or: *You're right. I recently met some new friends, and they have been hanging out late every Saturday evening, so it's been a challenge to get up on Sunday morning.*

- This response is going to take a whole different conversation to the others. Now you have his *why* and can move the conversation forward in the right direction.

Of course, if his answer reveals a personal struggle, it's important to empathise with that and to see how you can help him. Your best response may be "*Dave, I am really sorry to hear about your...*". This would be a classic opportunity for a "moment of disproportionate influence" when Dave realises that you care more about him than the issue or just getting the job done. If you just focus on his late-coming, you will probably lose a team member, and possibly a relationship.

If you show genuine care and compassion, you'll gain a whole new level of trust and commitment. This is relational leadership 101, but someone who is not committed to Loving Well will rarely create such significant moments.

At this point, you have now created safety, accurately shared the facts that you were aware of, and have received any clarification you need of facts that you were previously unaware of. Now the third step is to express your preference and/or expectations as clearly as possible.

Thirdly: Express your PREFERENCES or expectations clearly

This step focuses on being clear about what you want going forward. The win at this stage is to express your preference and expectation clearly, specifically, and respectfully. The best phrase for doing this is simply: *I would like it if...* or *I would prefer that...*

It's one thing to talk about what happened in the past, but you also need to establish what you want in the future. Often, we know what went wrong, but we are not that good at expressing how we want it to go well. Usually, we have a complaint but then are not clear about the solution or what we would prefer. The more clearly you can articulate that, the better the outcomes will be.

In the situation with Dave, you could say: *Dave, my* (or even better, use "our" referring to the team) *expectation is that all team members arrive on time when they are serving on the team. If you are running late, I would prefer that you let me know by text or phone call that you will not be here by the time we are due to start.*

Of course, when you are leading someone, or they are your employee, you may want to express an expectation rather than just a preference. *I would prefer you to be on time* is not what anyone is going to hear from their boss! However, even if you have the authority, the way you make the expectation clear will make a significant difference to your relationship as well as the outcome.

An Example: Paul and Philemon

There's an interesting example of this in the New Testament letter to Philemon. In this letter Paul has a challenging request to make to Philemon, asking him to receive Onesimus as a brother. This isn't as straightforward as it seems, because Onesimus was Philemon's former slave who had run away and now become a follower of Jesus.

Paul Engages Well by creating safety first, starting his letter with *"To Philemon our dear friend and co-worker"*, [78] Then he raises the issue like this: *"Therefore (Philemon), although in Christ I could be bold and order you to do what you ought to do, yet I prefer to appeal to you on the basis of love."* [79]

Wow. Paul could have demanded action by virtue of his position of authority, but instead, he chose to *"appeal on the basis of love"*. Guess which approach would have produced the better results? I think this would have been one of those "moments of disproportionate influence" and it would have been so fascinating to have a second letter to Philemon to hear what amazing fruit came out of the reconciliation between this now-saved runaway slave and his former master. We'll need to ask them one day...

Whether you are a boss, leader, parent, spouse, pastor or coach, take a leaf out of Paul's book here and "appeal on the basis of love".

There's one more step to take, and this one should follow straight after you have stated your preference and/or expectation clearly, accurately and respectfully.

Fourthly: Negotiate AGREEMENT

At this final step you must ask: *Dave, so can you agree that...?*

This is so important because to move confidently forward into the future, you want to be sure that the other person has understood your stated preference or expectation, and that they agree to commit to doing as you have agreed.

The point is that expectations and preferences must always be communicated AND mutually agreed upon for them to be valid and before they can be expected. Often, we expect things from those around us that we never explicitly expressed, and which they never agreed to. That's not fair, is it?

I might have an expectation that my wife Ali brings me breakfast in bed every day, but communicating that, and getting her agreement on it is a very different thing! Never assume that there is agreement. Ask for it. This puts the responsibility into the other person's hands and gives them a chance to weigh up their response and commitment to change.

> Never assume that there is agreement.
> Ask for it.

In Dave's case, if the real reason for his lateness was his job loss and subsequent travel challenges, he may respond with something like: *I understand why I need to be on time and want you to know that I am committed to being on the team and arriving on time. However, I need you to understand that I take three different buses to get there, and at the moment it is just challenging to work out how long that takes.*

You may respond: *Dave, I understand that and appreciate your commitment. Can you agree to let me know as soon as you can by text or phone call when you realise that your bus journey is taking longer than expected?* Now you are negotiating based on facts and preference or expectations. Doing this thoroughly will build genuine hope for future improvement, and you will leave the meeting with much greater confidence in how you will work together going forward.

And what if Dave shows up late again without letting you know? Then it's an opportunity to state the facts again and say: *Dave, I'm puzzled that you didn't let me know as we agreed. Can you tell me what happened?* Who knows, he may have been robbed of his phone on the second bus!

A TIP: To ensure that this last step is as effective as possible is to confirm what you agreed in writing so that you can refer back to it in the future should it be necessary. This can be formal or informal as appropriate. Perhaps even just a quick email with something like: *Hi Dave. It was good to talk today. Again, thanks for being on the team* (reinforce safety). *It was good to understand your side and agree that...*

Mastering The Art of Engaging Well will help you speak to just about anyone about just about any issue that is polluting a relational climate you're in.

How this has helped Ali and I

I'll give you one more personal example. In London we have a small garden, and I am responsible for the lawn part of it. Ali looks after the flowers. One thing that irritated me is when Ali watered her flowers with the hosepipe and then left it lying on "my" lawn all day, resulting in those unsightly hosepipe marks all over the grass. At first, I would say nothing and just pick the hosepipe up, albeit with a bit of a huff. But then I learnt *The Art of Engaging Well*. So I start with creating safety: *Ali, I love you and appreciate how stunning the garden looks.*

Then I express a preference: *Ali, because of the ugly marks that the hosepipe makes on 'our' lawn, I would prefer if you reel the hosepipe away after you have used it to water the flowers. Can you agree to that?*

Now it's time to negotiate, and she responds: *I understand that, but you know that the hosepipe reel is old and cranky, and it is really a struggle for me to roll it up when I am finished.* Now I either have to buy a new hose pipe reel or compromise, so I reply: *Ok, I understand that. How about you just pull it off the grass onto the paving area, and I will roll it up when I come into the garden. Can we agree to that?* Great solution, don't you think? (And no, I did not send her an email to confirm this!)

Whatever crucial conversation you need to have, I hope that this four-step process will help you to Engage Well. Learn. Practise. Review. Repeat. Growing in this Art is worth every bit of the effort.

You may well be asking some "but what about" questions at this stage, including:

What about when the other person is not cooperative?
Of course, it won't always result in reconciliation or resolve, but *"as far as it depends on you, live at peace with everyone."* [80] I suggest that you always take responsibility for doing your part as well as possible, and continue to do that no matter what the response.

What about when there has been significant conflict and emotions are running high? Will this still work?
That's a great question, and that's what the next chapter is about when we look at *The Art of Fighting Well.* This will build on the same framework, but add the heart and skills needed to address times of conflict, disagreement and high emotion.

Before we go there though, there is one more question we must all answer about *The Art of Engaging Well*, and that is *Why don't we?*

WHY DON'T WE HAVE THE CONVERSATIONS WE NEED TO HAVE?
We can probably all identify at least a few crucial conversations that we need to have, but for some reason haven't done so. We need to ask why we don't have these types of conversations quickly and well? What's stopping me? What's hindering this in our organisation, team, family or church? What's keeping us from Engaging Well? Let me ask you to

consider two fears as reasons why we don't: The fear of outcome reaction, and the fear of rejection.

The fear of outcome reaction

This is the result of previous attempts at addressing issues that went horribly wrong. You tried to engage but got such an adverse reaction from the person or the group, that you now accept the pollution as the new normal, rather than having to face the same negative reaction again. When this happens, those who don't want to Love Well have succeeded in controlling and manipulating the climate to keep from being faced with their own insecurities and the dysfunctional environment they are in. Intimidation and manipulation are allowed to rule. You know that this fear is operating when you are aware of some "no-go" areas that are taboo to talk about. You want to, but the fear of outcome reaction causes you to shrink back and tolerate the problem, rather than bring it up and risk creating an even larger one. You can measure the health of a relationship or organisation by the number of things you believe you can't talk about.

The fear of rejection

This second reason we don't have these conversations is when you are more concerned about what others think of you, than you are about what is true and right. Then you find yourself compromising what you value in the hope that you will be accepted. When this fear is in operation, there will never be what we crave in a relationship, which is real intimacy, or being fully known.

It seems that at a young age we start to believe a myth that we often must choose between telling the truth and keeping a friend. This causes us to hide who we really are and what we feel, but deep down we wonder whether we would be rejected if they really knew how we felt (if we had that crucial conversation). This fear will keep your relationships stuck, shallow and superficial. You may want to talk about things, but you don't, because you can't bear the thought of not being liked.

So those are two reasons why we don't. Getting back to the pollution in the air analogy that I used at the beginning of this chapter, these two fears are like powerful weather fronts that control the local climate, and when these are operating, your relational climate will be very difficult to improve. As you consider these two fears, please take some time to work through the "Think and Talk it over" section at the end of this chapter, reflecting on how this relates to you and your relational environments.

CONCLUSION

This *Art of Engaging Well* is not easy to master, but with a good dose of commitment and practice it will have a significant impact on your relational climates.

I hope I've put across how important this is and given you some tools to have the crucial conversations you need to have, with hopefully much better outcomes than before. As you commit yourself to growing and applying this Art, the pollution in your relational environments may begin to dissipate, and you might be amazed at the new level of flourishing that will result.

Earlier I said I'd end this chapter by telling you what happened when my friend hadn't had a salary review or a raise for three years and wanted to leave the company where he was working to get a better salary elsewhere but had never spoken to his boss about it. Well, after I'd coached him in *The Art of Engaging Well*, I challenged him to make an appointment with his boss to have this conversation. I called him a couple of weeks later and asked how it had gone. He confirmed that he had done it and had followed the four-step process:

1. **Safety:** *I have enjoyed working here.*

2. **Facts:** *It's been three years since I had any formal salary review or increase.*

3. **Preference:** *I would like us to set a formal appointment next week to speak about my job and my salary.*

4. **Agreement:** *Can you agree to that?*

It worked. They had the meeting and he stayed on with the company - with a significant salary increase! It's a few years later now, and he is still there and very happy working for them. All it took was *The Art of Engaging Well*. It addressed his current concern and also set a precedent for future healthy, honest and productive conversations. It changed his relational work climate in the workplace. I believe that you can have similar results as you learn and apply this Art.

Of course, it will always take the other person (his boss in this instance) to respond well, too, but even if they don't, it is still a much healthier way to conduct any relationship than ignoring the problem or simply walking away.

To Engage Well is to Love Well.

Let's grow in doing that well.

Remember the process of Engaging Well:

1. Create Safety

2. Engage with the Facts

3. Express Preferences or Expectations

4. Negotiate Agreement

Pause to think and talk about The Art of Engaging Well:

⇒ What is the one thing that you found most relevant or helpful in this chapter?

⇒ On a scale of 1-7, how good are you at initiating crucial conversations?

⇒ Think about a recent situation when you were deliberate in tackling an issue with someone, but it didn't go well. Why was this and what have you learnt from the experience?

⇒ Evaluate whether a "fear of outcome reaction" or "fear of rejection" operates in your relational environments. What caused this, and what is one thing you can do to overcome this particular fear?

⇒ What is one crucial conversation that you are aware of that you need to have in the next week or two? With whom? About what? When will you have it?

⇒ In response to the truth in this chapter, what is the one thing you can do differently to grow in Loving Well?

The Art of Fighting Well

*Because we will fight, and need to learn
to fight for the sake of relationship*

E ven the best of climates are at times threatened by vicious storms and destructive typhoons. How we anticipate, prepare, and react makes all the difference to the damage a storm will leave behind.

We *will* have conflict.

We *will* disappoint one another.

We *will* have differences of opinion.

We *will* have disagreements. Sometimes very sharp ones.

Offence *will* come.

The question is not *whether* we will fight, but only *how* will we fight.

No relationship comes with a storm-free guarantee, but I am convinced that there is a lot we can do to storm-proof our relationships. How we handle conflict will either build or break our relationships. It will either deepen or damage the bonds we have with others.

To Fight Well is to engage in a situation of conflict between two or more people in a healthy way that values the relationship (and honours God).

The opposite of Fighting Well is to fight dirty, which is to handle conflict in a way that has little regard for relationship, by using destructive words and actions.

Learning to Fight Well is vital to sustain and strengthen any relationship, but sadly we don't often do it very well, and there are many reasons why. In this chapter, we will learn the heart and skills to change the way we fight and learn to Fight Well more consistently. Let's be honest. This is something we all need. Parents. Siblings. Friends. Spouses. Partners. Colleagues. Christians. Churches. Neighbours. Even nations. There is way too much dirty fighting going on, and like a storm it leaves destruction, debris and dark clouds in its wake, spoiling what could be beautiful flourishing relationships.

MAKE CONFLICT YOUR FRIEND

Another decision I made at the New Decisions Seminar I mentioned previously is that *conflicts build bridges to better understanding others, and I face these conflicts gladly.*

Conflict is not a bad thing in a relationship because it often brings to the surface that which is already lurking beneath, so dealing with it well will deepen your relationships. Many team-building strategies include activities that intentionally attempt to surface the conflict that the team members have not even been aware of or have not been willing to face. As uncomfortable as these moments may be, if handled well they will result in much improved relational climates.

A few years ago, I was in such a situation with a team of leaders that I get to work with. The facilitator led us through a conflict-surfacing exercise and asked us to share anything negative we noticed in the way the team operated. A few people shared, and then it was my turn. I said: *I notice that whenever we speak about difficult matters relating to finances, someone on the team tends to change the subject or tries to make light of the situation, and we don't actually address the issues raised.*

In response, some tried to change the topic. Some denied it. Some got defensive. Some shifted uncomfortably. I tried to explain what I meant. There was misunderstanding. Defensiveness. There were some raised voices. Even a few tears. Then understanding. Then acceptance. And apologies. And when it was over, we were a better team for it, and have since then gone on to have some incredibly productive meetings over the years, including those about money matters.

Some people have the idea that for a relationship to be right, there should be no conflict. So, when conflict does arise, they conclude that the relationship must be wrong, and they turn away, continuing their search for perfection.

They want to live in a perpetual honeymoon, but life is sadly not like that. The moonlight and roses invariably turn to daylight and dishes, and we realise that neither we nor the other person, is perfect. The real problem is that the real problem is often right inside us, so wherever we go, there we are! What we really all want is to find a place where we are loved despite our imperfections. We want to be fully loved even though we are fully known, with our good, bad and even our ugly. This is exactly what we can experience when we Fight Well, because when we come out on the other side of conflict with our relationship intact, it confirms to us that we have found such a place of acceptance.

> What we all want is to fully loved even when we are fully known.

We will fight, but when we Fight Well, we find a very special prize waiting on the other side. Conflict *can* build bridges to better understanding others, so decide to put conflict to work for the sake of deepening your relationships.

Now let's look at a few things you can do to develop your ability to Fight Well:

1. Engage Well

To Fight Well you will first need to be wholly committed to *The Art of Engaging Well*, and to follow the four steps of the

Engaging Well process. Do you still remember these from the previous chapter?

1. Create _____

2. _____

3. Express _____

4. _____ Agreement

I must warn you though that this is easier said than done when the emotional temperature is turned up in the heat of the argument. Like a tired boxer swinging their arms widely in the hope of somehow landing a punch, we very easily lose our composure, and with it our ability to Fight Well. All four of the Engaging Well steps need to form the basis of our approach, and the more you stay committed to them, the more well you will fight.

2. Choose the prize you are fighting for

What you are fighting for, will determine how you fight. The prize you are fighting for will determine if you will fight clean or dirty.

The prize of a dirty fight is to win the argument, even at the expense of relationship. The prize of Fighting Well is a resolution for the sake of strengthening the relationship.

> What you are fighting for will determine how you fight.

When a fight does break out, it's important to keep in mind what is at stake and what you are fighting for. Consider these:

The issue: There's the issue that needs to be addressed and resolved. Who did what? This is obviously important, but often not nearly as much as it is made out to be. Make sure that you place the right value on this as a prize. How important is it really? What would you give up to be right? A dirty fighter fights to be right, but to Fight Well is to fight for the relationship.

> One of the hardest things in the world is to be right and not hurt other people with it - Dallas Willard

The relationship/s: Jesus commanded us to *"love one another".*[81] It's not a suggestion. It's imperative. This calls us to care much more about the relationship than about the issue. If you ever do sacrifice a relationship to be right about an issue, you'd better be prepared to explain yourself to Jesus! One practical tip for keeping the relationship central is to keep the issue in front of you and don't allow it to come between you. You may even use a physical object like a pillow to represent the issue you are talking about, putting it to the side of you, and not between you.

The testimony of Jesus and his church: For those who are followers (and representatives) of Jesus, there is something even more important at stake: The testimony of Jesus whom you confess as Lord, and the reputation of his body, the church. The way we fight, and what we fight for, either makes Jesus attractive or unattractive to others. As a Christian, you're never off duty from being his representative. Your instruction is clear: "*Whatever you do or say, do it as a representative of the Lord Jesus, giving thanks through Him to God the Father.*" [82] I implore us to hold the testimony of Jesus and his church in very high regard as we do our fighting.

There's a lot at stake when you fight, so make sure that you choose the right prize to fight for. Being right, while losing the relationship, is rarely a satisfying outcome.

3. Recognise your old coaches

We tend to fight in the ways we were taught to fight. Through examples, role-models, and experiences, we've all been influenced, or "coached" to fight in certain ways and tend to instinctively fight just as it was modelled it to us. Some of these coaches taught us well, but sadly, some did not.

Don't underestimate how your family background has influenced the way you respond to conflict. What we saw and experienced with our parents has a significant influence on us, either positively or negatively. In some families, conflict was dealt with in a healthy way that valued relationships and resolved the issues. In others, conflict was avoided at all costs. In some families, everyone wore their hearts on their sleeves, and everything was open to debate. Sometimes very loud debate! What happened in your home will have shaped your current fighting habits to some extent, either positively or negatively. Deep down in our souls, we make decisions about these things at a young age, and it is only with a good dose of self-awareness that we can recognise any dirty fighting patterns that we have adopted.

Learning to Fight Well will possibly require you to recognise your coaches and consider which ones to keep hired, and which ones to fire. Honour those who taught you well and forgive those who did not.

Pause and consider:
⇒ Where did you learn to fight like you do?
⇒ Who are you thankful to for teaching you to Fight Well?

4. Unlearn some old moves

We all have different fighting styles, and need to ask ourselves: Does the way I fight really deliver the prize I am seeking? Does the way I tend to fight really show a high regard for the relationship, or not?

Like a professional boxer who will review the footage of his previous fights to spot and learn from his mistakes, we too should do our best to identify the dirty fighting tactics that we are prone to use in the heat of the battle. These will always hinder us from getting the prize we're fighting for, so we should be totally committed to unlearning these bad moves and learning new ones.

But now is the time to get rid of anger, rage, malicious behaviour, slander, and dirty language. Do not lie to one another, since you have put off the old self with its practices.[83]

To get even more practical, I've listed several common dirty fighting tactics below. Each of these are against the rules for Fighting Well:

- ☐ Giving the Silent treatment
- ☐ Lecturing
- ☐ Blaming
- ☐ Attacking
- ☐ Condescension
- ☐ Threats (Words/actions)
- ☐ Physical violence
- ☐ Name calling. *You are...*
- ☐ Sarcasm
- ☐ Walking away / Withdrawal
- ☐ Placating
- ☐ Avoiding
- ☐ Shouting
- ☐ Using *always* & *never*
- ☐ Passive-aggressive behaviour
- ☐ Lying
- ☐ Exaggeration
- ☐ Belittling
- ☐ Dredging up the past
- ☐ Adding new issues to the conflict

I'm sure that you will agree that none of these is helpful to Fighting Well. They do nothing to promote proper resolution and relationship building and if they are part of the way you fight, they will always hinder you from getting the prize you're fighting for.

Pause and Consider: Have a look through the list of dirty fighting tactics again and identify which three are the ones you most default to and will need to change to start Fighting Well.

Remember: You are only as strong as you are honest. And faith can't fix what you won't face.

5. Prepare yourself well before any fight

If you don't prepare well, you will probably end up fighting dirty. During conflict situations, emotions have a way of taking over the agenda and before you know it your intentions to Fight Well have been hijacked. To avoid this, it's a good idea to prepare yourself by taking some time to reflect on some key questions before meeting to address the issue at hand, such as:

> **What am I feeling about this situation?** Do the iceberg exercise and try to articulate what your emotions really are. Angry? Sad? Disappointed? Frustrated? Hurt?

> **What value has been violated to cause me to feel this way?** For example, if a friend has lied to you, your

feelings of anger or disappointment may not just be because of the lie, but because you value truth and honesty, and that has been violated. A part of your conversation will need to be explaining your value to your friend and making it clear that you expect your friendship to honour that value in the future.

Your preparation could include writing down your responses to these questions, and what you want to say for each of the four steps of the Engaging Well process.

Preparation may also include sharing the above with a confidant or counsellor (but please not with the whole wide world). Talking it through and getting another perspective can be very valuable to help you prepare and Fight Well.

6. Get help from God. Pray!

For the believer, there is always help available for relational conflicts. God is love, and he specialises in reconciliation. Just remember though that he loves the other person just as much as he loves you, so don't expect him to take sides. He is for you, and also for the other person. The best thing to do is to start by asking for help for yourself and asking him to help you love the other person well. A part of that may require your forgiving them, which we will look at in the next chapter on *The Art of Forgiving Well*.

When you come to God in preparation, it may be helpful (and very challenging) to read through what Jesus taught in the book of Matthew:

You have heard the law that says, 'Love your neighbour' and hate your enemy. But I say, love your enemies! Pray for those who persecute you! In that way, you will be acting as true children of your Father in heaven. For he gives his sunlight to both the evil and the good, and he sends rain on the just and the unjust alike. If you love only those who love you, what reward is there for that? Even corrupt tax collectors do that much. If you are kind only to your friends, how are you different from anyone else? Even pagans do that. But you are to be perfect, even as your Father in heaven is perfect.[84]

Wow. Ouch.

Pray for them. It's a great way to get God's perspective on the other person or persons involved and also on the issue at hand.

After this you may also read these challenging words of the Apostle Paul to the Christians in Rome, taken here from The Message Translation:

Don't hit back; discover beauty in everyone. If you've got it in you, get along with everybody. Don't insist on getting even; that's not for you to do. "I'll do the judging," says God. "I'll take care of it."[85]

There's *beauty in everyone*. Every person is created in God's image. Every person has equal value. This is so difficult to see when you are in the heat of a fight, and that's why preparation is so necessary. Once you see others as God sees them, you will treat them with much greater dignity and respect, which is the foundation of Fighting Well.

Perhaps a final word of warning from Paul's letter to the Galatians will give a knock-out blow to any leanings we have towards dirty fighting:

> *For the whole law can be summed up in this one command: "Love your neighbour as yourself." But if you are always biting and devouring one another, watch out! Beware of destroying one another.*[86]

Biting one another.

Devouring one another.

Destroying one another.

Let's not do that.

Instead, let's love each other well, by Fighting Well.

One reality about fighting though: No matter how well you do it, in most cases, you will also need to practice *The Art of Forgiving Well*. That's what the next chapter is about.

To Fight Well is to Love Well.

Let's grow in doing that well.

Yes, we will fight, but the question is:

How will we fight?

How are you fighting?

Pause to think and talk about The Art of Fighting Well:

⇒ What is the one thing that you found most relevant or helpful in this chapter?

⇒ Would your family and friends say that you are generally a dirty fighter or one who Fights Well? Why would they say that?

⇒ Look at the list of dirty fighting tactics again. Do any of these apply to you?

⇒ In your mind review your last situation of relational conflict. What did you do well? What could you have done better to Fight Well?

⇒ In response to the truth in this chapter, what is the one thing you can do differently to grow in Loving Well?

The Art of Forgiving Well

*Because we mess up, and will often
need to forgive and be forgiven*

T o Love Well requires us to Forgive Well. *"Love does not keep a record of wrongs."* [87] But how do we really do that well?

I'm sure that you have been on the receiving end of a poor *"I'm sorry"* apology. There did not seem any real resolution to what had happened, and you just did not feel that they meant it.

Forgiveness is almost always required to make right when something has gone wrong in a relationship. But how do we do that well? That's what we will look at in this chapter. We'll go beyond the simplistic *I'm sorry* to understand the heart and learn the skill required to Forgive Well.

It's often said that not forgiving is like drinking a cup of poison and then expecting the other person to die of it. But where there is an existing relationship that has been affected, true forgiveness is not just about getting rid of the poison of unforgiveness from your own heart. It also includes a desire for reconciliation of the broken relationship. This does not mean that forgiving someone will always lead to reconciliation. That obviously also depends on the other person's response.

It's important to understand that to forgive only requires one person, but reconciliation will require both parties to want it and work at it. Also, it does not mean that everything is magically reset to how it was before. Forgiveness is given and received, but trust is to be earned, or re-earned if it has been broken.

Dallas Willard gives this challenging insight about the necessity of not just forgiving, but also pursuing reconciliation, if it is possible to do so. He describes that as *"a choice to resume relationships, in the light of good to be realised, after some violation of moral trust that has had significant harmful effects on those who are doing the forgiving. It is decided, by the one who forgives, that the good to be realised by resumption of the relationships—by no means saying the relationships are to be just the same as before the violation—is not to be sacrificed to the gratifications of resentment and retaliation".* [88]

Of course, often the offence, injustice, or injury was caused by a stranger, or even a now deceased person. In such cases, there is no relationship to reconcile as part of Forgiving

Well. The point here though is that where a relationship has been severed through something that requires forgiveness, a concern for the restoration of such relationship is a vital part of Forgiving Well, and that should guide our attitude and actions in the process.

It's a high standard, I know, but it's the one Jesus set for us, as we'll see below. It's always good to remember that we are often the ones on the receiving end of forgiveness, and in those cases, we surely would want to embrace this as the standard of forgiveness.

Consider these challenging instructions from Scripture:

> *Make allowance for each other's faults, and forgive anyone who offends you. Remember, the Lord forgave you, so you must forgive others.*[89]

> *Always be humble and gentle. Be patient with each other, making allowance for each other's faults because of your love.*[90]

> *Get rid of all bitterness, rage, anger, harsh words, and slander, as well as all types of evil behaviour. Instead, be kind to each other, tender-hearted, forgiving one another, just as God through Christ has forgiven you.*[91]

> *"Just as God in Christ forgave you."*

Did you get that? *"Just as."*

This is the basis and the source of our ability to forgive others.

We can give forgiveness because we have received forgiveness. Forgiveness is giving to others what we have ourselves received from God.

Jesus told a few stories of people who were forgiven what they owed, but then didn't forgive others.[92] They hadn't understood this *"just as you have been forgiven"* principle, so they could never give or receive forgiveness.

When Jesus was hanging on the cross, looking down through bloodied and swollen eyes on the blaspheming crowd and on those who had tortured him and hung him there, he prayed his final famous prayer, declaring: *"Father, forgive them, for they know not what they do."* [93]

> We can forgive because we have been forgiven.

The *"them"* is not just the Jewish rulers and the Roman soldiers who were about to bring him to his brutal end. The them is us. All of humanity. Our sin crucified Jesus. He died in our place for our sin and now offers forgiveness to everyone everywhere.

On the basis of his forgiving us, he taught his disciples to pray *"Forgive us our sins even as we forgive those who sin against us"*. [94]

Our forgiveness of others is always *"as God in Christ forgave us"*. Only once you really understand this can you be *"quick to forgive"*.

Before we look at *how*, let's acknowledge that forgiving is not always easy. It mostly takes great faith to forgive. There was a time when the Apostle Peter asks Jesus: *"Lord, how often should I forgive someone who sins against me? Seven times?"* Jesus shocked him by replying: *"No, not seven times, but seventy times seven!"* [95]

"Lord, increase our faith!" [96] is how Luke records the Apostle's response to this challenging standard. It's not easy, but it is possible, only *"because God in Christ first forgave us"*. [97]

Now let's get practical about how to Forgive Well. There are two key aspects of this:

1. How do you give forgiveness to others well?
2. How do you ask for forgiveness from others well?

We will consider these separately, starting with how to forgive others well. I'm sure that you have had many opportunities that required you to forgive others for what they did. I'm also sure that you have realised that doing this *well* is also a lot more complex than just saying: *OK I forgive you.*

So here are a few thoughts to help us to Forgive others Well:

HOW TO FORGIVE OTHERS WELL

I believe that a good place to start is by acknowledging that not all "sins against us" are equal. I think it's helpful to understand and agree that there are small things, and bigger things, and then really big things to forgive, and each requires a different response to forgive appropriately. Let's look at these in three categories of Small offences, Significant wounds, and Life-Shattering injustices: [98]

1. Small Offenses

If you can't distinguish between big and small issues, you're probably always going to have issues. I believe that one trait of maturity is to know what things in life to hold loosely, and what to hold more tightly. Getting angry and upset about everything will probably prevent you from getting angry and upset about the things that really do matter. A pizza that was delivered ten minutes late surely does not warrant the same response as finding out that someone has lied to you?

One characteristic of love is that *"Love is not easily angered"*. [99] That means that some things should simply not bother us as much as they do.

> Some things should simply not bother us as much as they do.

I have often been surprised at some people's overreactions at small things, even finding out years later that someone was upset with me because I did not greet them well enough once upon a time.

The way to deal with forgiving minor offences is to simply let go of your negative feelings and thoughts against the person and move on. Some things are just not worth spending any more emotional energy and time on.

If you are finding yourself having responses that are disproportionate to a given situation, getting upset about something that is minor (it happens), then use it as an opportunity to practise *The Art of Growing Up* and *The Art of Feeling Well*.

Explore why you feel so upset at the person. Why are you so easily offendable? Why has this irritated you so much? Is there something else that you haven't addressed through a Crucial Conversation, and now this minor thing is the so-called straw breaking the camel's back?

Christian, if you bring minor offences to Jesus, don't be surprised if you hear him respond with a challenging: *Really? You are really upset about that?* Or he may say: *Come on. Stop sweating the small stuff. Let's go change the world!*

Yep, I really think he'd say that.

2. Significant Wounds

There are small things, and then there are bigger things. When a friend betrays you. When a child lies to you. When someone gossips about you or breaks your confidence. When you find out your spouse is watching porn.

One cannot expect these kinds of offences to just be easily forgiven and forgotten. They break trust and bruise emotions, and mess with what we believed about people, so they require resolution and healing.

Forgiving Well in such cases is not easy and will be a process. *Just forgive them and move on* is not going to be enough, and that is ok. Jesus promised that *"Blessed are those who mourn, for they will be comforted."*[100] Mourning is a process that includes fully facing our feeling about our loss (or in this case, the pain experienced), accepting that it happened (don't deny the facts), and coming to a place of restored wholeness or comfort.

Forgiving Well in this category is not easy, but it is possible. And necessary. Staying stuck in unforgiveness is never a healthy option. At some point we will need to do what we know is right and good and best, and *"forgive even as God in Christ forgave you"*. Jesus is our example and because he forgave us and those who mistreated him, we too can find the strength and grace to forgive.

In Matthew chapter 18 Jesus gave his disciples some guidance on how they could approach such situations, including the following steps:

Go: There comes a point in the processing of legitimate hurts that interaction with the person involved is necessary to move forgiveness further. First, go in private (not on social media!). If necessary, go with someone else who can mediate.

Go Well: Use *The Art of Engaging Well* and *The Art of Fighting Well*. Have a Crucial Conversation. Be bold. Be Brave.

Go to reconcile: Remember that Forgiving Well includes the goal of restoration of the strained relationship. *"If possible, so far as it depends on you, live peaceably with all."* [101]

Let it Go: It's wonderful when the relationship can be restored. To forgive only requires one person, but reconciliation requires both to want it. Some will, and some won't. When this happens - and sadly it will - let it go and get on with your life. Trust them into God's hand and *"Don't insist on getting even; that's not for you to do. I'll do the judging," says God. "I'll take care of it".* [102] And he will take care of you as you trust him.

3. Life-shattering Injustices

These are major tragedies: A drunk driver kills a family member. Adultery. Rape. Treason. False accusations. Being swindled of your life savings.

In these circumstances it's important to understand that forgiveness doesn't mean releasing perpetrators from the consequences of their actions. It does not mean that someone who has broken the law gets let off scot-free. That is not in your individual authority to decide.

Is it "an eye for an eye", or "turn the other cheek"?

Reading the Bible, you may be confused whether your response should be *"an eye for an eye"*,[103] or *"turn the other cheek"*[104] when you are the subject of a life-shattering injustice. Here's how I interpret this for us today: *"Turning the other cheek"* is an instruction to you as an individual to respond to another individual who has wronged you. *"An eye for an eye"* was not an instruction to an individual, but to a community, on administering justice. Therefore, it is my responsibility as an individual to forgive anyone who has wronged me, no matter how heinous the crime, but this does not mean that the law will not take its full course and *"punish those who do wrong"*,[105] which is the role of civil government in the New Testament. I forgive, and civil government punishes according to the law. I propose to you that that's the way it should work.

Undeniably though, Jesus taught his followers a radically different way to the world: *"But I say, love your enemies! Pray for those who persecute you! In that way, you will be acting as true children of your Father in heaven."* [106]

Love your enemies. This is not easy. It is hard work and can only be done with deep revelation of what God has first done for us and for all - including for those who have been the cause of life-shattering injustices towards us. Only those who know that they have been forgiven much can forgive much.[107] There is no greater demonstration of love than extending mercy and grace to the one who does not deserve it. To do so is to *"act like children of your Father in heaven"*.

Mary Johnson's inspiring example

She faced a life-shattering injustice when her twenty-year-old son was murdered at a party. Seventeen years later she forgave her son's murderer, and now lives as his neighbour.

Understandably, the forgiving process was extremely painful for her. She says: *"The root of bitterness ran deep, anger had set in and I hated everyone. I remained like this for years, driving many people away. But then, one day, I read a poem which talked about two mothers—one mother whose child had been murdered and the other mother whose child was the murderer. It was such a healing poem all about the commonality of pain and it showed me my destiny."*

After the murder, Mary recalled: *"Unforgiveness is like cancer. It will eat you from the inside out. It's not about the other person. Me forgiving him does not diminish what he has done. Yes, he murdered my son. But the forgiveness is for me."* [108]

Mary now dedicates her time to "From Death to Life", an organisation she founded that uses healing and reconciliation to end violence between families of victims and those who have caused harm.

FAITH TO FORGIVE WELL

It will take great faith to Forgive Well in such life-shattering situations, but when we do find the power to do so in Jesus, something that was meant for evil and destruction can be turned around for good in a profound and beautiful way.

Whatever small, big, or bigger thing you have faced or are facing in your own life, I pray that you will find the grace to forgive those who have sinned against you, even as you, in Christ, have been forgiven. Once you have said *I forgive you,* it means that you have made a conscious decision to cancel their debt owed to you. You no longer require it of them. You don't bring it up any longer, even in the heat of new conflict. You have set them free to rebuild trust with you.

Remember: Trust needs to be earned, not demanded. Forgiveness lays the groundwork for a process of reconciliation to start. That's how we Forgive Well.

NOW, HOW TO ASK FOR FORGIVENESS FROM OTHERS

If you are like me (or just human), I am sure you have needed to do this at least a few times in your life. Like me, I'm sure you have had someone that you are asking to forgive you reply with: *You're NOT sorry!* or *You don't really mean that!* This is because often we'll just say something like: *I'm sorry* and think that it's done. I've said it and they must accept it. Well, *I'm sorry* is a start, but it only deals with your own feelings. It doesn't yet acknowledge the other person's offence and how what happened made them feel.

Let me show you that there is more you can do to Forgive Well. Here's how you can go beyond *I'm sorry*:

1. **Add "for" to your "I'm sorry"**
    So you are sorry, but sorry for what? Do you even know? Are you clear what you really did? (Remember: Engage with the facts.) Adding *for* identifies and acknowledges the issue and communicates that you are clear about exactly what you did.

    I am sorry for lying to you about...
    I am sorry for forgetting our meeting.

I am sorry for assuming that about you.

I am sorry that I forgot about...

And, by the way, be careful of ruining a good apology with an excuse...

2. **Add: "I understand how what I did made you feel..."**
This acknowledges the feelings that your actions caused. Just a caution: Don't assume you know how the person feels. Use this line only if they have already said how it made them feel or add it once they have told you. You can, however, always say: *I am sure that I have disappointed you,* or *I know that I have hurt you.* The important part is to empathise with their feelings, as well as with the facts of the issue.

3. **Ask: "Will you please forgive me?"**
Don't assume forgiveness because you've said that you are sorry, and don't ask this question until you have covered all the above. But once you have acknowledged the facts and feelings, ask them clearly in a way that gives them the choice to say yes or no. This empowers them to do what only they can do. You cannot demand forgiveness. It is their choice, and yours to ask for, not demand.

4. **Ask: "What can I do to make it right?"**
This is an offer of restitution if it's needed. It is about making right as far as possible any wrong done. If you stole something, give it back. If you broke something,

have it fixed. If you gossiped about someone, go to everyone you spoke to and tell them that you lied or were a jerk. You get the point. It's important that this is not grovelling, but a genuine expression of being willing, as far as possible, to pay the cost of making right any damage or hurt you caused.

Those are some thoughts about how to ask for forgiveness well. When next you need to ask someone to forgive you, go over these again and do them. I bet you'll get a better result than previously.

As we end this chapter, take a moment to commit yourself to this Forgiving Well instruction from the Apostle Paul:

> *Make allowance for each other's faults, and forgive anyone who offends you. Remember, the Lord forgave you, so you must forgive others. Above all, clothe yourselves with love, which binds us all together in perfect harmony.*[109]

To Forgive Well is to Love Well.

Let's grow in doing that well.

> Be kind to each other, tender-hearted, forgiving one another, just as God through Christ has forgiven you.

Pause to think and talk about The Art of Forgiving Well:

⇒ What is the one thing that you found most relevant or helpful in this chapter?

⇒ Consider the following:

• Is there anyone you need to ask for forgiveness?

• Is there anyone you need to forgive?

• Is there any small offence you just need to let go of so you can get on with living your life?

⇒ In response to the truth in this chapter, what is the one thing you can do differently to grow in Loving Well?

The Art of Functioning Well

Because relationships flourish
when we each do our part

I believe that as humans, we have two great needs: The need to belong and the need for significance. We all need to be able to say: *I am loved*, and: *I matter.*

The Art of Functioning Well focuses on this latter need for significance. Survival of the fittest is simply too low a bar to set for human existence. Consuming is never as life-giving as contributing. We were created for more than that. We were created on purpose for a purpose. To be fruitful and multiply. That's not just about making babies, but about making a difference beyond ourselves.

According to the Oxford dictionary, to function is defined as: "An activity that is natural to or the purpose of a person or thing."

You were created on purpose for a purpose. Every person you know was created on purpose for a purpose.

To Function Well is to positively contribute to the relational environment that you are in, according to your own unique gifts. A community Functions Well when every person's gift is honoured and empowered to contribute to its purpose. The way we function and allow others to function has a profound effect on our relational climates.

Consider the flourishing that happens when we Function Well, as taught by the Apostle Paul to the church in Ephesus: *"As each part does its own special work, it helps the other parts grow, so that the whole body is healthy and growing and full of love."* [110]

> *When we all Function Well, it helps everyone else to grow.*
>
> *When we all Function Well, our community is healthy.*
>
> *When we all Function Well, love grows.*

The above verse is preceded by this statement: *"He (God) makes the whole body fit together perfectly."*

You fit. You matter. I matter. We all have a purpose and a part to play, and when we play that part, we contribute to the flourishing of our relational environments.

The question is: How do we Function, and will we Function Well?

Unfortunately, many relational environments are filled with too much:

Insecurity
Comparison
Competition
Pride
One-upmanship
Jealousy
Control
Rivalry
Manipulation
Indifference
Etc.

Where any of these are operating, they spoil our relational climates and lead to sad alternative ways of functioning:

1. **Under-functioning** is when you are functioning below your capacity and calling.

2. **Dysfunctioning** occurs when one does not function according to one's own unique gifts but tries to be someone or something else.

3. **Over-functioning** is when you are doing for others what they can and should be doing for themselves.

This is not Functioning Well!

Imagine how different it would be if instead we functioned with the attitude that Paul instructed the Christians in Rome and Philippi to have:

I give each of you this warning: Don't think you are better than you really are. Be honest in your evaluation of yourselves, measuring yourselves by the faith God has given us. Just as our bodies have many parts and each part has a special function, so it is with Christ's body. We are many parts of one body, and we all belong to each other.[111]

Don't be selfish; don't try to impress others. Be humble, thinking of others as better than yourselves. Don't look out only for your own interests, but take an interest in others, too.[112]

Paul continues this instruction to the Philippians by holding Jesus up as our example:

You must have the same attitude that Christ Jesus had. Though he was God, he did not think of equality with God, as something to cling to. Instead, he gave up his divine privileges, he took the humble position of a servant.[113]

Jesus became a servant to be a blessing to all, but not all accepted him. Where he was acknowledged for who he was, and his gift was received, there life flourished. Where they only recognised him as the carpenter's son,[114] they missed out on the blessing he could have been to them as the Son of God, their Saviour. Where he was rejected, they missed out on the greatest gift ever available to man. Where they received him, they received from him the gift of eternal life.

A CULTURE OF HONOUR

This has been called a *culture of honour*,[115] which states that when you accurately identify God's gift in someone, and wholeheartedly receive it from them, you release the blessing of God's gift in them to yourself and into your relational environment.

The Apostle Paul connects love, honour and our functioning together like this:

> *Don't just pretend to love others. Really love them. Hate what is wrong. Hold tightly to what is good. Love each other with genuine affection, and take delight in honouring each other. Never be lazy, but work hard and serve the Lord enthusiastically.*[116]

> *Take delight in honouring one another.*

How amazing would it be to function in a relational environment with such a culture of honour? Everybody loved. Everybody valued, appreciated, and celebrated. Every gift recognised and empowered to contribute to the purpose of the whole. Every person filled with a sense of significance.

Surely we all flourish when we Function Well like this?

> *It's incredible what can be achieved if no one cares who gets the credit.*

Let's explore a few aspects of Functioning Well.

CELEBRATING DIFFERENCES

We have different personalities, gifts, talents, strengths, weaknesses, and preferences. How we deal with our differences greatly impacts whether our relationships will flourish. We are quick to expect others to understand us, but often slow to try to understand them. Often our default is to expect others to become like us. We want others to accept the way we are but are often slow to accept the way others are, and this does not help us to Function Well.

There are various responses we can have towards differences in others: Reject. Tolerate. Accept. Celebrate.

Reject: Here we don't accept the difference and make it our mission to try to change the other person (This rarely works, especially in marriage!)

Tolerate: Here we resign ourselves to the fact that they are as they are and try to live with it. There is no synergy in this.

Please note I do not mean that we should tolerate or accept behaviours and attitudes that are destructive, manipulative or suchlike. When these are present, then *The Art of Engaging* Well is needed.

Remember: be a *peacemaker*, not just a *peacekeeper*.

Accept: Here we see the benefit of the difference and begin to function together.

Celebrate: This is the attitude that will cause flourishing in a relational climate. Now we are not just focused on how we benefit, but on the blessing that the other person is to us with their differences and uniqueness. We celebrate *them*, not just what they do for us. We find joy at how they enrich our relational environment. People contribute all they are when they know that all that they are is celebrated, not just tolerated, or even appreciated.

Pause and consider: In your key relationships, how are you currently rejecting, tolerating, accepting, or celebrating differences? What one thing could you do to start celebrating the differences of one specific person close to you?

UNDERSTAND YOUR "G.R.A.C.E.D. SHAPE"

It's one thing to hear that "you are a special part", but which part are you? How can you best contribute? Where do you fit? What is your purpose? To Function Well you will need a certain level of clarity and confidence about these questions.

First, recognise that you *do* have gifts: *In his grace, God has given us different gifts for doing certain things well.* [117] God created you like he wanted you, with your personality, strengths, weaknesses, abilities, talents, etc. Everyone has gifts, but not everyone has the same gifts.

To the Old Testament prophet Jeremiah, God makes this powerful declaration: *Before I shaped you in the womb, I knew all about you. Before you saw the light of day, I had holy plans for you.* [118]

God shaped you and graced you with gifts according to the plans he has purposed for your life: *For we are God's masterpiece. He has created us anew in Christ Jesus, so we can do the good things he planned for us long ago.* [119]

To help you more practically understand your part and purpose, try this exercise below to determine what I call "your G.R.A.C.E.D. SHAPE". Take some time to write down your answers to each section before you continue:

G is for your GIFTS
From what you or others have recognised, complete the sentence: *I have the gift/gifts of/to* _____ (List at least 3 things)

R is for your ROMANCE
What do you love and enjoy doing? What are you passionate and enthusiastic about? What do you care deeply about? What "moves" you to tears or action?

> **TIP:** If you find yourself a little stuck on this point, you may find it helpful to write what I call an *"I love list"*. Just take a blank piece of paper and start writing all the things that you love, and love doing: I love walking in the evening. I love movies. Pizza. Helping people. Teaching. Organising. Providing. Kids. Sunsets. Singing. Fixing things. Hosting guests. Creating. Etc. Don't overthink it, just write, and then step back and see any trends, or recognise things you have written that you have buried or neglected.

A
is for your ABILITIES

What do you do well? What are you good at? What do you do in regular work/hobbies? What training have you had? (Your lack of ability will not exclude you from a ministry but will influence the level of initial involvement.)

C
is for your COMMUNITY

You can't separate your purpose from your people. Who are the people you have committed to walk with? Who do you love to hang around with? Who is going where you want to go?

E
is for the EVIDENCE from your life

What is the "fruit" of your life? What have you done? Where have you been involved before? What went well, and what did not? What is it that you do that blesses or helps people? What do people comment positively about to you? What makes you feel "alive" when you do it? Also consider: What drains you?

> What makes you feel "alive" when you do it, and have done it?

D
is for your DREAM/DESTINY

Do you have a dream that is pulling you forwards?

Do you have a sense of God's calling on your life? Like a puzzle piece, you need the bigger picture to know where you fit.

Pause and consider:

Once you understand your G.R.A.C.E.D. SHAPE try to identify three possible ways by which you are or can begin serving and functioning in your relational environments.

1.

2.

3.

Admittedly this exercise is easier for some than for others. When teaching on this topic I usually hand each attendee a piece of a puzzle taken from a world map. I then ask them whether they can determine where in the world their puzzle piece fits by looking at their piece. If your piece has "Hawaii" written on it, then that's an easy answer. But it's a lot more difficult if your piece is just all blue sea and could be anywhere in the world's vast oceans! Seriously though, whether it is an easy thing for you to identify or not, finding where you best fit and starting to function is the first step to Functioning Well. Note that I said, "best fit", not perfect fit. That's because neither you nor those around you are perfect. Just in case you thought otherwise.

From the above exercises you may also conclude that you have been functioning as a square peg in a round hole. For some reason you have got into a rut doing what is draining you and there's no joy or fruit resulting from your functioning. If this is the case, then it's time to have some Crucial Conversations with whom you are working or serving and start a process to transition to where you will Function Well according to your gifts and purpose.

BEING FREE TO FUNCTION WELL

Besides knowing where you fit, there are often other hindrances that will hold you and others back. The world longs and needs for you to Function Well, but the enemy fears that and will do whatever he can to oppose and quench you being you and expressing God's gift in you to your world. Here are some tactics he will use against you:

1. **The fear of failure: "I can't"**

   The fear of failure results in passivity. Because you believe that you will fail, and that failure is bad, you don't even try. But there is no progress without failures along the way. Failing does not make you a failure. It just helps you to eliminate one more way not to do a thing and takes you one step closer to success. Like Yoda of Star Wars said: *"The greatest teacher, failure is."* Learn from failure, don't let it limit you. The greatest failure for most people is the failure to start.

2. **Fear of rejection**: "What will others think of me?"

   This operates when you believe the lie that you *are* what you *do*. When your identity is tied too tightly to your activity. You are not a human doing, but a human being. You *are*, no matter what or how well you *do*.

   > You are a human being, not a human doing.

3. **Intimidation:** "Who do you think you are?"

   At the church service in Cape Town where Ali and I were commissioned to come to London to start a new church, there was a "prophetic word" shared with us, which declared: *"When you get to London, they will challenge you, asking: 'Whose business are you on?' And you will answer: 'We are on the business of the King!'"* We were being prepared for facing intimidation that would intend us to shrink back and stay small. This is what intimidation will do to you if you don't overcome it with a sense of purpose and courage. Whose business are you on?

4. **Pride:** *"This is below me."*

To Function Well is synonymous with serving well. *"Even the Son of Man came not to be served but to serve others."* [120] If serving is below you, then go back to *The Art of Growing Up,* and do that. Service is greatness, not just the way to greatness.

5. **Inferiority:** *"Who me?"*

The Bible is littered with people who did not think that they had what it takes. Think Moses. Or Gideon. Let God alone define you. Believe who he says you are, and what he says you can do. And do it in his strength.

6. **Comparison:** *"Do I match up?"*

"Comparison is the thief of joy", said Theodore Roosevelt. Fuelled by social media, comparison is a scrounge of our day that continually bombards us with how others seem to be more and have more than we do. To be free to Function Well requires you to run in your own lane and to believe that your life is uniquely deeply meaningful to others. There is no one like you. You have no rivals. You have a unique contribution to make. In a healthy relational environment, we do inspire and encourage one another to be the best version of ourselves that we can be, but we never compare with an attitude of determining a pecking order or positioning.

7. **Perfectionism:** *"It's got to be perfect before it's worth it."* Perfection isn't the goal, it's part of the problem. If your standard is perfection, then this will be your problem. As Salvador Dali famously said: *"Have no fear of perfection - you'll never reach it."*

8. **Procrastination:** *"I'll do it some other time."* There are seven days in a week, and someday is not one of them. Often, we procrastinate because of one of the above reasons. The best thing to do is what could be another chapter in this book: *The Art of the Start.* You'll be surprised what you can do once you break the resistance of that initial inertia.

> *"The best time to plant a tree was twenty years ago. The second best time is now."* - Chinese proverb

Pause and consider: Are any of these stopping you? Which one, or ones? Perhaps this next truth will help you.

> You were created on purpose for a purpose.

CARRY YOUR LOAD, AND CAST OFF YOUR BURDENS

Writing to the Galatian Christians, the Apostle Paul gives some key instructions that relate to our Functioning Well:

Carry one another's burdens; in this way you will fulfil the law of Christ. For if anyone considers himself to be something when he is nothing, he deceives himself. Let each person examine his own work, and then he can take pride in himself alone, and not compare himself with someone else. For each person will have to carry his own load.[121]

Carry each other's burdens. A burden is a weight or trouble you are not created to bear on your own. This can be related to your purpose, or your pain. Burdens are what you are carrying, but can't cope with: Guilt, shame, regret, condemnation, and lies.

The word *load* here is from the Greek word *phortion* which refers to that which must be carried by the individual. It is something personal and hence is not transferable, i.e. it cannot "be shifted" to someone else. [122] Your load is what you are graced and gifted to carry. It's your calling. Your task. Your place to take. Your part to play. Your role to fulfil.

> Your load is what you are graced, gifted and called to do in this season.

Paul continues with this encouragement:

Let us not become weary in doing good, for at the proper time we will reap a harvest if we do not give up. Therefore, as we have opportunity, let us do good to all people, especially to those who belong to the family of believers. [123]

I like to see this as *sowing good.* We don't just *do good* but we *sow good,* and we reap what we sow. The Greek word for *doing good* is *kalós,* which means "attractively good; good that inspires (motivates) others to embrace what is lovely (beautiful, praiseworthy)" [124] When we do good by carrying our loads, it inspires others to carry theirs, and the result is something beautiful and praiseworthy. That sure sounds like flourishing to me!

AN EXAMPLE OF FUNCTIONING WELL FROM THE EARLY CHURCH

In the life of the early church, we get an insightful glimpse into a community that learnt to Function Well, with some extraordinary results. We read this in the book of Acts, chapter six, where the church was experiencing some exciting growth:

In those days when the number of disciples was increasing...

All success has its own practical and relational challenges, and to sustain healthy growth will require some very intentional application of *The Art of Functioning Well.*

Here's what happened next, with some comments from me:

...the Hellenistic Jews among them complained against the Hebraic Jews because their widows were being overlooked in the daily distribution of food.

- Note: Complaints are a type of feedback. Instead of rejecting, the wise person will use *The Art of Listening Well* to identify the kernel of truth in the complaint. Imagine what would have happened here if these leaders had rejected this complaint?
- Unmet needs and expectations are always a threat to a relational climate.
- We all want growth, but growth means change, and change often leads to relational tensions as the status quo is threatened. Next, we see how they responded to address these growing tensions:

So the Twelve gathered all the disciples together and said, 'It would not be right for us to neglect the ministry of the word of God in order to wait on tables. Brothers and sisters, choose seven men from among you who are known to be full of the Spirit and wisdom. We will turn this responsibility over to them and will give our attention to prayer and the ministry of the word.'

> Even if you think you can do everything, you cannot do everything well.

- The tendency when faced with needs and complaining, is to rush in and fill the gaps. That may stop the complaining but is usually only a short-term solution.

- What we see here is the leaders recognising that for the community to Function Well, everyone needs to do their part.

- They said "no". Knowing their priorities enabled them to say no to the needs that others could fulfil. To be able to say no, you must know what you need to say yes to.

- STOP trying to do *everything*. Even if you think you can do everything, you cannot do everything well.

- STOP over-functioning: Don't do for others what they can and should do for themselves. It's actually selfish. Over-functioning may make you feel useful and indispensable, but it will keep others immature and dependant, and rob them of their opportunity to Function Well.

They chose seven... They presented these men to the apostles, who prayed and laid their hands on them.

- Here we see gifts identified, and then being accepted by the group.

So the word of God spread. The number of disciples in Jerusalem increased rapidly, and a large number of priests became obedient to the faith.

- This is the result of Functioning Well: Because they functioned well, it resulted in continued growth and flourishing all round.

- In fact, there was even more flourishing that resulted from this, because we see that at least two of those who served tables, Stephen, and Philip, went on to become mighty leaders in their own right. How well you function with seemingly small things will determine whether you are ready to be entrusted with greater things.

As I consider this account it seems clear to me that when *The Art of Functioning Well* operated, it caused their whole relational climate to change and allowed many to flourish.

I firmly believe that we can experience the same climate change results as we commit to doing our part and accept and champion others doing their part.

As each part does its own special work, it helps the other parts grow, so that the whole body is healthy and growing and full of love.[125]

We Love Well when we Function Well.

Let's grow in doing that well.

> In his grace, God has given us different gifts for doing certain things well. [117]

Pause to think and talk about The Art of Functioning Well:

⇒ What is the one thing that you found most relevant or helpful in this chapter?

⇒ Reflecting on the G.R.A.C.E.D. SHAPE exercise, what would you say are three possible areas where you are best suited to contribute to your community now?

1. _____

2. _____

3. _____

⇒ In what ways are you using your gifts and talents to serve?

⇒ Is there something that is preventing you from Functioning Well? What is it, and what first step could you take to addressing this hindrance?

⇒ In response to the truth in this chapter, what is the one thing you can do differently to grow in Loving Well?

The Art of Living Loved

Because we can only give love
when we have received love

We've heard that without love we are nothing. It's also true that without first receiving love, we have no love to give.

God is love.[126]

We love, because he first loved us.[127]

Love your neighbour, even as you love yourself.[128]

In the Scriptures, husbands are commanded to *"love your wives, **even as Christ loved** the church, and gave himself for her"*.[129] How can a man possibly do that? Where do I find the ability to love like that? To do that would mean I would have to be like God, who is love. How is that even possible?

Well, it isn't possible. Or rather, it isn't possible in my natural ability. I don't have that kind of love in myself. Not for my wife, nor for my neighbour, or my enemy. The only way to love like God loves, is to do so with his love, and the good news is this, that *"God's love has been poured out in our hearts through the Holy Spirit who was given to us"*. [130]

God's love is also the basis for us being able to *"love ourselves"*. This isn't a self-love based on an overactive ego, but a humble realisation that because God first loves me, I also can love myself.

I believe that all we need to Love Well has been made fully, abundantly available to us by a Creator God who is love, has demonstrated love, and pours out love into every heart that makes room for it. When you have received this love, you can give it to the world around you. I believe this is the key to being able to love like God loves. If you have it, you can give it. His love for you and in you enables you to love others like he does. But to really Live Loved, there are a few things that you must know and believe about God's love in order to receive it fully:

Firstly, God *is* love.

He doesn't just have love, he is love.[131] It is his nature. When you come to him, you will find love. It's who he is and what he does. This is so important, because what you know and believe about him, will determine how you relate to him. Whether you will run to him, or from him.

> *What you know and believe about God will determine how you relate to him.*

Secondly, God has demonstrated his love.

He has proven his love for the world and for you through the life, death on the Cross, and resurrection of Jesus Christ.

But God showed his great love for us by sending Christ to die for us while we were still sinners.[132]

While we were sinners. He loves us in spite of us. We didn't earn his love, nor deserve his love. So, when in doubt, look back and know his love through this sacrifice, for there is no greater love than to give your life for another. As unworthy as we may be, or feel to be, the good news is that God doesn't define us by our actions, but by his love. Not because of what we have done, but despite what we have done.

> The truth of the Gospel is that our situation is far worse than we ever imagined, and God loves us far more deeply than we ever dreamed. - Tim Keller [133]

Thirdly, God loves everybody.

Yes everybody. *"For God so loved the world..."*.[134] That means everyone, everywhere, over all time. And you. God doesn't just love good people, but all people.[135] You have never met anyone whom God loves more than you, nor less than you. This is so important because someday you will not feel worthy of his love, and that's the time to remember that he does love everyone, including you.

Fourthly, God loves you uniquely

That means you have no rival for his love. You are not in competition with others for a portion of his love and affection. Think about it: A parent does not love one child more than the other but loves each child in a unique way. You can't ask me: *Which of your two daughters do you love more?* That's impossible to answer, because Amy is uniquely special to me, and so is Abby. Ranking them is impossible. To be unique is to be "without rival". You are not competing with anyone else for God's love. To him you are irreplaceable. You don't need to impress him, just come to him as yourself.

> God loves each of us as if there were only one of us.
> - Augustine

Fifthly, God's love transforms us.

There is a powerful account in the Gospel of Luke where a broken woman gate-crashes a party at a Pharisee's house where Jesus was a guest. She desperately wanted help, and she'd heard how Jesus had treated other sinners with kindness and forgiveness. So she risks ridicule, rejection and embarrassment as she makes her way into the house towards Jesus. When she gets to him, the scene is described like this:

> *Then she knelt behind him at his feet, weeping. Her tears fell on his feet, and she wiped them off with her hair. Then she kept kissing his feet and putting perfume on them.*[136]

Wow. This must have been a pretty awkward scene for most of the party guests. But this is what love, and seeking love, does.

Love makes us do things we would never ordinarily do.

Love leads us across dividing lines.

Love overcomes our fears and inhibitions and pride.

Love motivates radical generosity.

Love leads us to where we find true wholeness.

Commenting on this incident, Jesus says that she has *"loved much"*, and as they part ways, he through his love says to her: *"Your faith has saved you; go in peace."* [137]

Jesus loves her. Jesus saves her. Jesus gives her peace.

The word *saved* here is from the Greek *sozo*, which means "to preserve, rescue, save from death, or keep alive". In addition, Jesus declares *peace* to her, which is God's gift of wholeness, when all essential parts are joined together to form a perfect whole. God's love in Christ caused a massive relational climate change for her, and it can do the same for you and everyone whom you know.

We are all her

The truth is that we are all like this woman. We are all broken and bruised and rejected and empty in our own unique ways, and we all desperately need healing and restoring in our souls. We too are sinners desperately needing grace and forgiveness. And like this woman, we can - you can - come to God and receive a love that restores in every way.

COMING HOME TO GOD

If you really want to know what to expect when you decide to turn to God for help, the best place to look at is one of the well-known stories Jesus told about the "Prodigal Son". It's about a son who demanded his share of his inheritance from his father, and upon receiving it, he leaves home and wastes it all in an ill-judged pursuit of happiness. Eventually, when he hits rock bottom, he "repents" and makes a life-changing decision to return home.

To repent means to change your mind and heart, resulting in a change of actions. He changes his mind about sin, and, crucially, also about his father. Sin had promised him everything, but now he sees that it had deceived and nearly destroyed him. Previously he'd viewed his father as one who restricted and limited him, but now he has a revelation of his father's goodness, even to his servants. With this new mindset and change of heart he is now ready to change his ways and go home.

But what kind of reception would he get when he got there? Would his dad put the dogs on him? Would he be turned away? Rejected? Would he be put to work until he had paid back all he had wasted? Jesus' original listeners would have been sitting on the edge of their seats as they anticipated this part of the story, which they knew was explaining to them how God the Father would react to them, should they decide to turn their backs on their sin and turn their lives back over to him. How would God receive them? Here's how Jesus tells this part:

So he returned home to his father. And while he was still a long way off, his father saw him coming. Filled with love and compassion, he ran to his son, embraced him, and kissed him.[138]

This was an incredible unexpected twist to the tale. No judgment. No condemnation. No grovelling required. He receives a passionate warm welcome, through which we get a front-row view of the amazing grace of God available to every one of us.

But there is more. Even after this passionate reunion, the Prodigal still says, *"I am not worthy to be called your son".* [139] You see, as wonderful as passionate moments are, they are not enough. We need more than passion. We need a promise. We need more than hugs and kisses. We need a covenant. We need a seal put on this love.

Here's how Jesus continues the story to show this:

But his father said to the servants, 'Quick! Bring the finest robe in the house and put it on him. Get a ring for his finger and sandals for his feet. And kill the calf we have been fattening. We must celebrate with a feast, for this son of mine was dead and has now returned to life. He was lost, but now he is found.'

So the party began.[140]

The father not only gives the son a hug and a kiss, but also a robe, a ring, new sandals, and a prepared sacrifice. Each of these have significant symbolism to show the covenant that God makes with those who come to him to receive his love through Jesus Christ. He gives him the best robe, which symbolises the covering of sins and the believer's "righteousness" and "justification" in Christ. It declares that in Jesus, *I am just-as-if-I-had-never-sinned.* By faith alone, through grace alone, in Christ alone, I am restored to be in right standing with God.

> We need more than kisses. We need a covenant.

He also gives a ring, symbolic of our belonging. *I am his.*

And he gives us new sandals. Where previously we had, like the prodigal son, walked away, we are now empowered to walk a new walk as loved and fully restored sons and daughters of God. *I walk in his truth. I now follow Jesus.*

And all this is possible through the prepared Sacrifice: Jesus himself, who on the cross demonstrated his great and lavish love for us, and through his resurrection guarantees that his is a love that will last forever. Even death cannot part you from God's love.

By placing your faith in Jesus Christ, you can receive the love of God, not just as a feeling, but a fact. Not just as a moment, but as a mark of confident assurance on your life that declares *I am one loved by God!*

Here's the great promise to all who will believe and receive Jesus as Saviour and Lord:

But to as many as did receive and welcome Him, He gave the authority (power, privilege, right) to become the children of God, that is, to those who believe in (adhere to, trust in, and rely on) His name.[141]

As a child of God the Father, you can also know this great promise about his enduring, unchanging love:

So now I live with the confidence that there is nothing in the universe with the power to separate us from God's love. I'm convinced that his love will triumph over death, life's troubles, fallen angels, or dark rulers in the heavens. There is nothing in our present or future circumstances that can weaken his love. There is no power above us or beneath us—no power that could ever be found in the universe that can distance us from God's passionate love, which is lavished upon us through our Lord Jesus, the Anointed One![142]

Because of what God has done through Jesus Christ, nothing in all the universe has the power to separate you from the love of God!

THE POTENTIAL FATHER PROBLEM

Knowing God as "perfect loving father" is Biblical and wonderful. However, this can be a difficult concept for those who had negative experiences with their natural fathers or other key authority figures.

In such cases, the word "father" may evoke all kinds of bad memories and emotions. You may respond, *If God is like my dad was, then no thanks!*

Pause and consider

If you do struggle to accept God's love, it may be worth considering whether you are relating to God through the lenses of any negative father experiences. These can be considered as "father wounds" (where we have experienced hurt, abuse, breaking down by fathers), or "father vacuums" (where we experienced the absence of all that a father should be).

As you identify and acknowledge these, and the associated feelings (use *The Art of Feeling Well*), invite God the Father to heal and fill these with His love and an understanding that you are His totally and completely loved son/daughter. It may also be helpful to speak to a friend or counsellor if you identify this as a real struggle in your life.

Also, please remember that our negative reactions to any of these (e.g. judgement, unforgiveness, bitterness) can be even more destructive than the original actions. Most of us at some point need to use *The Art of Forgiving Well* towards our fathers and other authority figures in our lives.

YOU ARE LOVED BY GOD.

God's Father love is wonderful to believe and experience. As the Apostle John declares:

> *See how very much our Father loves us, for he calls us his children, and that is what we are!* [143]

This is true, but the question is: Do you really believe it?

Do you experience God's love as a reality in your life?

SINGING THE GOOD GOOD FATHER SONG

One way to evaluate your true feelings about God as father is to consider how sincerely you can express these lyrics from the song "Good Good Father" by HOUSEFIRES II: (You may want to find the song on YouTube and take a few minutes to listen and reflect)

Oh, I've heard a thousand stories
Of what they think You're like.
But I've heard the tender whisper
Of love in the dead of night.
And You tell me that You're pleased
And that I'm never alone.

You're a good, good Father.
It's who You are, it's who You are, it's who You are.
And I'm loved by You.
It's who I am, it's who I am, it's who I am.

Oh, it's love so undeniable, I can hardly speak.
Peace so unexplainable, I can hardly think.
As You call me deeper still,
As You call me deeper still,
As You call me deeper still,
into love, love, love ...

RECEIVE GOD'S LOVE

How was that song experience for you? If you struggled with it, and you feel empty of love, the application of this Art starts by deciding to receive this love from God the Father through Jesus Christ.

If that's what you want and need, I invite you to pray this prayer below to God, and receive his love for yourself:

Heavenly Father,

I pray that from your glorious, unlimited resources you will empower me with inner strength through your Spirit — that Christ will live in me as I open the door and invite you in.

I believe that my roots will grow down into God's love and keep me strong.

May I have the power to understand how wide, how long, how high, and how deep your love is. May I experience all the extravagant dimensions of Christ's love.

Then I will be made complete with all the fullness of life and power that comes from you. [144]

Thank you!

The good news is that we can all come as we are, but we don't need to stay as we are.

We can receive God's love that forgives, restores, and transforms us. And because we have received his love, we can love others.

We love each other because he loved us first.[145]

You can love, because God first loved you.

That's what it means to Live Loved.

Let's live like that!

See how very much our Father loves us, for he calls
us his children, and that is what we are!

1 John 3v1

Pause to think and talk about The Art of Living Loved:

⇒ What is the one thing that you found most relevant or helpful in this chapter?

⇒ Do you accept as fact that God loves you, and demonstrated his love through Jesus Christ's birth, life, death, and resurrection?

- If not, what are your objections and questions?

⇒ Considering the part in the chapter about the "potential father problem", take a few minutes to consider if any of the statements below describe you:

☐ *I recognise symptoms of "father wounds" or "father vacuums" in my life and should consider receiving ministry and prayer for healing and restoration in these areas.*

☐ *I have judged my parents, instead of honouring them.*

☐ *I have not forgiven my father/mother/any authority figures in my past. I do so now. (See The Art of Forgiving Well)*

Please speak to a friend or counsellor if you need more help with any of these crucial issues.

⇒ In response to the truth in this chapter, what is the one thing you can do differently to grow in Loving Well?

Now: Live the Love

Because love can change everything

In this book we have explored ten powerful ways to change your relational climate, and I have proposed that if you start to put these Arts into practice, you will begin to see the relational climate change that is necessary for your relationships to flourish.

I really believe that, and I hope that you now feel that change in your relationships is not something that you just need to wish for, but that there really are ways you can bring it about. Relational climate change is possible.

One of the challenges we all face when wanting to change something is that the "to do list" can be very overwhelming, and because we can't change or do everything, we end up not changing or doing anything. So as I end this journey with you, I am going to list the ten Arts below again, and ask you to look over them and choose the three that you think would make the most difference to your specific relational situation. Once you have identified the three, I suggest that you go back over these chapters and start your climate change campaign with these as a priority:

1. The Art of Growing Up Well
2. The Art of Building Up Well
3. The Art of Feeling Well
4. The Art of Listening Well
5. The Art of Speaking Well
6. The Art of Engaging Well
7. The Art of Fighting Well
8. The Art of Forgiving Well
9. The Art of Functioning Well
10. The Art of Living Loved

So, have you identified your top three?

Will you commit to Loving Well by living these Arts?

Now:

Walk in love.[146]

Now that you know these things, blessed and happy and to be envied are you if you practise them [if you act accordingly and really do them].[147]

Think of yourself as an artist, and each of the ten Arts as a different colour on a palette that is available for you to use to transform the boring grey of any relationship into a beautiful precious masterpiece. It's an art to use the colours together, sometimes blending them, and skilfully applying them in the right amounts in the right place on the canvas that is your relational environment.

To be frank, it will not always be easy. Not everyone will respond to love with love. In fact, in some cases things will even seem to get worse before they get better, because to Love Well will threaten the status quo and disturb the comfort zones of those who have accepted a dysfunctional or toxic relational climate as their new normal. But please do not despair: Love will make a way. Love can transform. Relational climate change is possible. Love will win.

Here are your final instructions to help you Love Well:

> *Watch what God does, and then you do it, like children who learn proper behaviour from their parents. Mostly what God does is love you. Keep company with him and **learn a life of love**. Observe how Christ loved us. **His love was not cautious but extravagant.** He didn't love in order to get something from us but to give everything of himself to us. Love like that.*[148]

Keep *"learning the life of love"* from the One who has first loved you.

Be extravagant, not cautious. Let's love like that!

A CLOSING PRAYER FOR YOU

As we end this journey exploring *The Art of Loving Well*, I want to bless you with these two prayers adapted from the writings of the great Apostle Paul:

I pray that your love will flourish
and that you will not only love much but well.
I pray that you will learn to love appropriately.
That you will use your head and test your feelings
so that your love is sincere and intelligent,
not sentimental gush. [151]

I pray that the Master Jesus
will pour out his love so it fills your life
and splashes over on everyone around you.[152]

May you live and love like this,

because *To Love Well is to Live Well.*

To
Love Well
is to
Live Well

Thank you for reading!

I would greatly appreciate it if you could leave a short review on Amazon or wherever you bought this book and let me know the one thing that was most helpful to you.

About the Author

Wolfgang, or as he is affectionately known, Wolfi, is passionate about helping people to live well, love well, and lead well. He is married to Ali, together with whom he founded the Every Nation Church London in 1993. Wolfi also fulfils a strategic leadership role among Every Nation churches in Europe and internationally. He and Ali have two daughters.

Born in Namibia with German as his home language, he grew up in South Africa. He was not raised in a Christian home but became a Christ follower in his late teens. After university and working as a project manager for a large construction company, his life took a new trajectory as he answered a call to vocational ministry. This led him and Ali to hear God's call to start a new church in London, and in 1993, having never been there before, and knowing no one, they landed at Heathrow Airport with their "two backpacks and a vision". It's been an incredible adventure touching countless lives and nations through church planting, campus ministry and a passion to see the good news of God's amazing grace experienced by every person, and God's Kingdom come in every sphere of society.

Back in his youth he once ran a sub four-minute mile and has completed a couple of London marathons, but nowadays he prefers "board" meetings – especially snowboard and stand-up paddleboard meetings!

Further Resources & Connect

BOOKS

⇒ "DateTalk", a book for not-yet-marrieds which looks at *"(almost) everything you need to know about dating, relationships and sex."* (Available on Amazon, various retailers and Every Nation Churches)

⇒ "The Follow Course", an intentional three-part journey to help you grow as a follower of Jesus. Available to church leaders from Every Nation London.

ONLINE

⇒ Facebook page: *"The Art of Loving Well"*

⇒ Church Website: www.everynation.london

⇒ Blog: www.wolfinlondon.com

⇒ You can watch the "DateTalk" series for free on YouTube via 6x28-minute videos, as well as many other teachings.

⇒ Other social media via whatever is current when you read this!

TV

⇒ On www.tbnuk.org watch *"The Art of Loving Well"* programming as scheduled or via on-demand.

Endnotes

1. Luke 10:27; Strong's NT 2198
2. Philippians 1:9 The Message Translation
3. The Oxford English Dictionary
4. Strong's Word Study 4052. perisseuó
5. Ephesians 5:1-2 The Message Translation
6. 1 Thessalonians 3:12
7. Matthew 24:12
8. Article from The Harvard Gazette, referencing the study at www.adultde-velopmentstudy.org
9. John 13:34
10. 1 John 3:18 The Living Bible
11. 1 John 4:18
12. John 13:35
13. Philippians 1:10-11 The Message Translation
14. Jesus in John 15:13
15. 1 Thessalonians 3:12 NIVUK
16. 1 Thessalonians 3:12 The Message Translation
17. Proverbs 3:3-4 The Message Translation
18. Bob Dylan
19. John 13:34
20. 1 Corinthians 13:11
21. Ephesians 4:13-15
22. I first heard this line from Steven Furtick
23. Galatians 5:22-23
24. Galatians 5:19-21 The Message Translation
25. Romans 12:6
26. 1 Thessalonians 5:11
27. Jesus, in Luke 6:45
28. Proverbs 4:23 NIV
29. I highly recommend all their excellent resources, including the "Emotionally Healthy Skills Course" which introduces their view of "Exploring Your Iceberg", at www.emotionallyhealthy.org. Some of this book was definitely inspired by their resources.

30. Psalm 51:6 Amplified Bible

31. This was through the "New Decisions Seminar" by Juliana Bosma and Glenn Chapman, which is another excellent tool for inner healing and freedom through a process of identifying sources of negative patterns and lies, and displacing those by making new decisions based on truth.

32. Psalm 147:3

33. Isaiah 9:6

34. Derived from the Greek work "Eirene" - Strong's 1515

35. Psalm 147:3

36. Philippians 4:6-7 The Message

37. Philippians 4:6-7 New International Version

38. David Augsburger, in his book Caring Enough to Hear and Be Heard

39. Douglas Steere

40. Matthew 20:26

41. James 1:19

42. Stephen Covey, The 7 Habits of Highly Effective People

43. David Augsburger, in his book Caring Enough to Hear and Be Heard

44. Ephesians 4:14-15

45. Proverbs 18:21

46. Genesis 1, and Hebrews 1:3

47. Matthew 12:36

48. Ecclesiastes 3:7

49. Psalm 141:3

50. Proverbs 21:23

51. James 1:2

52. James 1:3-4

53. James 1:8

54. Luke 6:45

55. Proverbs 15:23

56. Proverbs 25:11

57. Proverbs 18:21

58. Ephesians 4:29

59. Ephesians 4:15

60. John 17:17

61. John 8:32

62. 1 Corinthians 13

63. John 1:17
64. Colossians 4:5-6
65. Ephesians 4:25
66. James 1:19
67. Numbers 6:24-27 NKJV
68. Romans 12:21
69. Psalms 19:14
70. Ephesians 4:15
71. Crucial Conversations, Joseph Grenny
72. Proverbs 15:1
73. 1 Timothy 1:3
74. www.vitalsmarts.com.au
75. Joseph Grenny, Crucial Conversations
76. Pete and Gerry Scazzero's Emotionally Healthy Skills Course
     - see www.emotionallyhealthy.org
77. John 8:32
78. Philemon 1:3
79. Philemon 8-9
80. Romans 12:18
81. John 13:34
82. Colossians 3:17
83. Colossians 3:8-9
84. Matthew 5:43-48
85. Romans 12:18-19 The Message Translation
86. Galatians 5:14-15
87. 1 Corinthians 13:5
88. From the article "Intentionality and the Substance of the Self"
     by Dallas Willard
89. Colossians 3:13
90. Ephesians 4:2
91. Ephesians 4:31,32
92. For example see Matthew 18:21-35
93. Luke 23:34
94. Matthew 6:12
95. Matthew 18:21-22
96. Luke 17:5

97. Ephesians 4:32
98. These three categories are similarly presented in Bill Hybels' book SIMPLIFY
99. 1 Corinthians 13:5
100. Matthew 5:4
101. Romans 12:18
102. Romans 12:19 The Message Translation
103. Matthew 5:38
104. Matthew 5:38-39
105. 1 Peter 2:14
106. Matthew 5:44-45
107. Luke 7:47
108. www.theforgivenessproject.com/mary-johnson-and-oshea-israel
109. Colossians 3:13-14
110. Ephesians 4:16
111. Romans 12:3-5
112. Philippians 2:3-4
113. Philippians 2:5-7
114. Matthew 13:55-58
115. Culture of Honour, by Danny Silk
116. Romans 12: 9
117. Romans 12:6
118. Jeremiah 1:5 The Message Translation
119. Ephesians 2:10
120. Matthew 20:28
121. Galatians 6:2-5
122. Strong's Concordance word study 5413
123. Galatians 6:9-10
124. Strong's Concordance word study 2570
125. Ephesians 4:16
126. 1 John 4:8
127. 1 John 4:19
128. Matthew 12:31
129. Ephesians 5:25
130. Romans 5:5
131. 1 John 4:8

132. Romans 5:8

133. A Tim Keller saying

134. John 3:16

135. Luke 6:35

136. Luke 7:36

137. Luke 7:50

138. Luke 15:20

139. Luke 15:21

140. Luke 15:22-24

141. John 1:12 Amplified Bible

142. Romans 8:38-39 The Passion Translation

143. 1 John 3:1

144. Adapted from Ephesians 3:16-19

145. 1 John 4:19

146. Ephesians 5:2

147. John 13:17 Amplified Bible

148. Ephesians 5:1-2 The Message Translation

149. www.willowcreek.org.uk/gls/

150. www.josephgrenny.com

151. Adapted from Philippians 1:9 The Message Translation

152. Adapted from 1 Thessalonians 3:12 The Message Translation

A final reminder:

To

Love Well

is to

Live Well

Printed in Great Britain
by Amazon

48078952R00121